*Louisiana Bicentennial
Reprint Series*

Louisiana Bicentennial Reprint Series

JOSEPH G. TREGLE, JR., General Editor

The History of Louisiana,
translated from the French of M. Le Page du Pratz
JOSEPH G. TREGLE, Editor

The Manhattaner in New Orleans:
Or, Phases of "Crescent City" Life,
by A. Oakey Hall
HENRY A. KMEN, Editor

Norman's New Orleans and Environs,
by Benjamin Moore Norman
MATTHEW J. SCHOTT, Editor

NORMAN'S NEW ORLEANS
AND ENVIRONS

NORMAN'S
NEW ORLEANS
and
ENVIRONS

Benjamin Moore Norman

Edited by Matthew J. Schott

Published for the
Louisiana American Revolution
Bicentennial Commission
by the
Louisiana State University Press
Baton Rouge

Library of Congress Cataloging in Publication Data

Norman, Benjamin Moore, 1809–1860.
  Norman's New Orleans and environs.

  (Louisiana bicentennial reprint series)
  Reprint of the 1845 ed. published by the author, New Orleans; with new foreword and new introd.
  Includes bibliographical references.
  1. New Orleans—Description—Guide-books. I. Title.
II. Title: New Orleans and environs. III. Series.
F379.N53N67 1976   917.63'35   75–21961
  ISBN 0–8071–0168–0

C74247

CONTENTS

FOREWORD

FOR THOSE who love New Orleans, there is a certain ineffable, bittersweet quality to any contemplation of her history in the three decades prior to the Civil War. This is particularly true of the mid-1840s, when Benjamin Moore Norman's *New Orleans and Environs* captured the surging optimism of a city convinced that it stood on the threshold of unparalleled commercial and metropolitan greatness. Panic years had receded, the bounty of the vast middle valley of the nation was again pouring through her precincts to the trade routes of the world, and awareness of the imminence of new economic dominion toward the Pacific stimulated already sharpened ambitions. "Queen City of the South," "Emporium of the West" her newspapers called her, emphasizing that still prevalent ambivalence as to precise geographic identification.

This certainty of great tomorrows gave New Orleans in the 1840s a restless vitality that overflowed into a host of civic improvements and activated a lively commitment to a life of sensate rather than intellectual concern. Assured of prosperity, invigorated by a population of diverse personality, the city could turn without nagging fears of profligacy to those attractions always ineluctable in its milieu: good food, good music, good conversation, good theater—in short, to the full enjoyment of life's pleasures.

In a real sense these years were the matrix of the city's character, fixing within it a spirit which would prevail even after malign fate had snatched away the full promise of economic ascendancy. This is the New Orleans we are able to recapture in Norman's sketch, with a sigh, perhaps, for unrealized grandeur, but with a compensatory recognition that possibly the very qualities which make the city so loved might well have perished had the vision of the 1840s become reality. Thus we are given one more glimpse of the richness of the tradition reburnished in these bicentennial commemorative reprints.

Matthew J. Schott, associate professor of history at the University of Southwestern Louisiana, is himself New Orleans born, with a particularly sharp knowledge of the city's later history which enables him to place Norman's work in proper focus. There is something essentially proper in the partnership: native and adopted sons celebrating a city which truly belongs to both.

JOSEPH G. TREGLE, JR.

INTRODUCTION

GUIDEBOOKS like Benjamin Moore Norman's 1845 publication *New Orleans and Environs* have an engaging quality, partly because the reader is easily led to a smug comparison of his own certain knowledge of later developments with the unbridled optimism of the community booster of times past. One expects to find in such volumes much hyperbole affirming that a particularly vigorous and farsighted city will one day become the greatest or next to the greatest in the state, upon the continent, or in the world. Norman predicted as much for New Orleans—a population of 300,000 by 1860, a doubled expanse of settlement by 1880, and a metropolitan area extending by 1900 from the Mississippi River to Lake Pontchartrain and embracing one million souls. With characteristic exuberance concerning future prospects, he begged posterity "to consider that our humble work" was the product of "the benighted age of steam!" (84–85)[1]

Yet enhancing one's interest in *New Orleans and Environs*, as well as its significance, is the awareness that at no other time in the city's history could the town

[1] This and other parenthetical numerical references hereafter cited indicate pages in *New Orleans and Environs*.

promoter more reasonably envision such a glorious ascendancy. The prediction of no less than Thomas
Jefferson, that the river port would be the greatest city
in the Western Hemisphere, seemed to many in the
process of realization. As Norman's guide appeared,
the city had recovered from the commercial setback
following the crash of 1837, the docks had assumed
their normal bustle, and J. D. B. De Bow, pronouncing
the slave-based cotton kingdom the strongest civilization on earth, was asserting that "no city in the world"
had "ever advanced as a mart of commerce with such
gigantic and rapid strides as New Orleans."[2] The new
St. Charles and St. Louis hotels, their elegant domed
rotundas dominating the business districts in the
American and French sections, testified to the prosperity and importance of New Orleans. In a day when the
Greek Revival style had triumphed, when hotels,
banks, and mansions had assumed the appearance of
temples, and when the slave societies of ancient times
were celebrated as models of refinement, it was hardly
immodest to think of New Orleans as entering a Golden
Age.

In American cities, it was typical for newcomers like
Norman and the Charlestonian De Bow to become the

[2] Cited in Richard C. Wade, *Slavery in the Cities: The South,
1820-1860* (New York: Oxford University Press, 1964), 6. Clement Eaton
has described the New Orleans-based *De Bow's Commercial Review of
the South and West*, which had been moved by its publisher from Charleston, as the "chief intellectual expression" of New Orleans. *The Growth of
Southern Civilization, 1790-1860* (New York: Harper and Brothers,
1961), 296.

most fervid community boosters. Having moved to the
Crescent City in 1837, Benjamin Norman approached
his new surroundings with the perspective of the
northerner. Born in Hudson, New York, on December
22, 1809, he worked as a clerk in New York until his
father's death left him heir to a bookstore in Philadelphia. In New Orleans he reentered the bookselling
business,[3] establishing the partnership Norman and
Steel on Camp Street in the burgeoning American business district above Canal. In the 1840s and 1850s he
operated Norman's Book and Job Printing Office at 16
Camp, advertised as a bookstore with "an extensive
and complete Printing and Bookbinding Establishment
where a variety of Printing and Binding is Executed."[4]

While Norman's business was listed in the city directories until 1860, all the major writing and publishing
ventures associated with his name appeared between
1843 and 1851. In addition to *New Orleans and
Environs*, these included a business directory, two
book-length rambles, two articles, a monthly journal,
agricultural almanac, and a series of schoolbooks.[5]

[3] *Appleton's Cylcopaedia of America* (New York: D. Appleton and Co.,
1888), IV, 531.
[4] *Norman's Agricultural Almanac for 1848*, ed. Thomas Affleck (New
Orleans: 1847), inside back fold, unnumbered.
[5] Norman's publications include *New Orleans Business Directory*
(1845–1846); *Rambles in Yucatan, or Notes of Travel Through the Peninsula* (1843); *Rambles by Land and Water, or Notes of Travel in Cuba and
Mexico* (published by Norman in New Orleans and by Paine and Burgess
in New York, 1845); "Rambles in the Swamps of Louisiana," *Arthur's
Magazine*, I (January, 1844), 9–12, reprinted in Eugene L. Schwaab and
Jacqueline Bull (eds.), *Travels in the Old South* (2 vols.; Lexington:
University Press of Kentucky, 1973), II, 302–309; "Two American Rid-

Rambles in Yucatan, published in 1843, and *Rambles by Land and Water, Notes of Travel in Cuba and Mexico*, which appeared in 1845, were Norman's most popular works. The enthusiastic response to the latter volume, published in the North in many editions, undoubtedly resulted from the interest centered in the area during the Mexican War. Norman based these books on a travel regimen conceived as an oddly contrived effort to recover from ill health. He had suffered an attack of yellow fever in 1841 during an epidemic which had also claimed the life of his wife, Emily.[6]

These travel books and an 1844 article, "Rambles in the Swamps of Louisiana," reveal Norman's interest in natural science, his concern with geographic and social origins, and his devotion to accurate description of the regions and their peoples. The rambles, as well as sections of *New Orleans and Environs*, express an especially keen interest in Indian anthropology (11–12) and agriculture (45–56). The books on Cuba and Mexico were undertaken as research on the subject of ancient civilizations. Admitting his lack of expertise in the field,

---

dles," in Robert Gibbes Barnwell (ed.), *The New Orleans Book* (New Orleans: n.p., 1851), 269–84; Norman's *Monthly Supplement* was apparently published for a brief period in 1846 and 1847, and copies may be found in the William S. Hamilton Papers, Louisiana State University Department of Archives and Manuscripts. The *Supplement* advertised the schoolbook series which included grammar, arithmetic, and history books and was commended by *De Bow's Review*, I (February, 1846), 191.

[6] *De Bow's Review*, I (February, 1846), 191; Schwaab and Bull (eds.), *Travels in the Old South*, II, 302. The death of Norman's wife is mentioned in the New Orleans *Bee* and the *Commercial Bulletin*, September 10, 1841.

Norman hoped that his study would stimulate interest on the part of antiquarian and historical societies.[7] From the vantage point of his bookstore, Norman undoubtedly read with fascination, but found unappealing, the current evolutionary theories preparing the way for the Darwinian synthesis. In an essay published in 1851 entitled "Two American Riddles," he rejected the "sceptical theory of the progressive generation of man," arguing from reasons of personal pride, reason, faith, and affections, as he explained, that he could not accept the idea that "man is but an improved . . . monkey, a civilized aurang-autang with his tail worn off or driven-in." The article maintained that the American Indians of his day had not evolved from the same race responsible for the ancient Central American ruins, but were, rather, a distinct and lower race of people.[8]

Norman's writing on the subject of agriculture dwelled on themes stressed in *New Orleans and Environs*, the need for crop diversification and limitation of cotton production, and the desirability of specialization of labor between cane growing and sugar manufacturing. *Norman's Agricultural Almanac*, published 1846–1848 and edited by Thomas Affleck, prominent promoter of scientific agriculture, advertised these ideas.[9] For a brief period in the 1840s, Norman published a journal, the *Monthly Supplement*, devoted primarily to agricultural news. In October,

[7] *Rambles by Land and Water*, v–viii.
[8] Barnwell (ed.), *New Orleans Book*, 269–84; quoted, 284.
[9] For example, *Norman's Agricultural Almanac*, 1848, p. 33.

1846, the journal announced that Norman was opening a depot for disbursement of printed materials on agriculture and horticulture. In 1847 *De Bow's Review* praised the "enterprising" Norman for distributing, free of charge or at cost, information of special interest to planters.[10]

On at least one other occasion, in 1846, *De Bow's Review* commended Norman, in this instance for his "industry" in "publishing valuable works."[11] Yet there is no record that Norman persisted in major promotional writing or publishing efforts after 1851, and little is known about his personal life in this or in the earlier period. On February 3, 1860, the New Orleans *Daily Picayune* commented in reporting the news of Norman's death at Summit, Mississippi: "He was unfortunate in business, however, and finally . . . with little left of the product of many years' labor, withdrew to an obscure spot in the country, apparently desirous of being forgotten by all his former associates and friends."

City directories and guidebooks, frequently melding common features, were typically among the first original books (as opposed to reprints) published on the urban frontiers of the United States in the early nineteenth century.[12] Norman's guidebook could have been inspired by any number of this type, though a few

---

[10] *De Bow's Review*, III (January, 1847), 90.

[11] *Ibid.*, I (February, 1846), 191.

[12] Blake McKelvey, *American Urbanization: A Comparative History* (Glenview, Ill.: Scott, Foresman and Co., 1973), 21.

examples are worthy of mention. One of the most famous was Dr. Daniel Drake's 1815 *Natural and Statistical View, or Picture of Cincinnati and Miami
County*, which in turn, it is reported, had been modeled
on James Mease's 1811 volume, *The Picture of
Philadelphia, Giving an Account of Its Origins, Increase, and Improvements*. Drake's piece on Cincinnati, circulated throughout the world, provided in addition to its boosterism a battery of statistical, ar-
chaeological, topographical, and climatological facts on
the small town and its environs.[13] *Gibson's Guide and
Directory of the State of Louisiana and the Cities of
New Orleans and Lafayette*, published in 1838, stands
out as having qualities that could have inspired Norman, though there are significant differences between
it and *New Orleans and Environs*. Most of Gibson's
larger volume is given over to a directory section, and
its organization and dispersement of statistical information make it more an almanac than a strictly defined
guidebook. Unlike Gibson's volume, Norman's excludes the directory and listing of local governmental
agencies and political functionaries, contains fewer
statistical summaries, and, with its more detailed description of physical landmarks, is more specifically for
the benefit of the visitor than for the resident New
Orleanians.

[13] Charles N. Glaab, *The American City: A Documentary History*
(Homewood, Ill.: The Dorsey Press, Inc., 1963), 43; Daniel J. Boorstin,
The Americans: The National Experience (New York: Random House,
1965), 115–22.

Between 1838 and 1845 other volumes incorporating
directory and guide sections appeared in New Orleans,
but because of its limited focus *New Orleans and Environs* has been identified by a literary historian as the
city's first guidebook.[14] The particular emphasis of
Norman's volume also sets it apart from Edwin L.
Jewell's 1873 *Crescent City Illustrated: The Commercial, Social, and General History of New Orleans*, considering the latter's dedication to "capitalists, immigrants, and the commercial world," and its greater
stress on individual businessmen and enterprises. As
was fashionable in the New South, half of Jewell's
pages are devoted to biographical sketches of prominent citizens, and the book reflects less of the compiler's
intellectual curiosity and genuine excitement about
municipal progress than his self-conscious desire to
flatter the city's commercial leadership. Another distinguished guidebook of the nineteenth century to
which Norman's may be compared is William H.
Coleman's *Historical Sketch Book and Guide to New
Orleans and Environs* of 1885. Published in New York
and prepared for the tourist, it incorporates aspects of
the directory, guide, and historical survey, with a preface by George Washington Cable recommending pieces
contributed to it by such luminaries as Charles Gayarré
and Lafcadio Hearn.

In a perceptive chapter on America in the first part of

[14] Albert Goldstein, "The Creative Spirit," in Hodding Carter (ed.),
The Past as Prelude: New Orleans, 1718–1968 (New Orleans: Tulane
University, 1968), 181.

the nineteenth century, Daniel J. Boorstin, having noted the role of guidebooks, states that "in upstart cities the loyalties of people were in inverse ratio to the antiquity of their communities, even to the point of absurdity." [15] Notwithstanding Norman's boasting about the tremendous growth foreseen for his adopted city, however, *New Orleans and Environs* is actually rather exceptional in its lack of exaggerated claims, a quality not surprising in view of the Crescent City's relative antiquity by American standards. Not a long-time resident of one of the "upstart" communities —rather a New Yorker in an old Creole domain— Norman took a politely critical glance at such examples of state and municipal backwardness as he found, most prominently the laggard pace in the development of public education and sanitation (43–44, 122, 165), and the absence of a public library (79–80). On the other hand, Norman's volume generally conforms to a pattern of proud civic commentary. The public accommodations, including the jails and workhouses, are seen as commendable (129–33); the crime rate is reported as incredibly low (78); poverty is ignored; embarrassments like slavery, vice, and mosquitoes are practically banished from the eye; and, against the recollections of most visitors during the period, the unhealthy climate is defended (45, 77).

Like *New Orleans and Environs*, city guidebooks of the nineteenth century usually were introduced by

[15] Boorstin, *National Experience*, 122.

lengthy descriptions of the geography and the history
of the region. Norman's guide follows this pattern,
emphasizing the natural environment's richness and
suitability for agricultural expansion and diversification (28–41). His historical survey, compared to the
early and mid-nineteenth-century works of François
Xavier Martin and Charles Gayarré, is hardly remarkable except perhaps for the degree to which his in-
terpretation of the Spanish and territorial periods expressed a contemporary Louisiana historiographical
consensus merging French, or anti-Spanish, and
American nationalistic biases (7–27).

Given its limitations as a secondary source for geog-
raphers and historians, and apart from its value as an
exemplar guidebook, *New Orleans and Environs*
provides a fascinating glimpse at various facets of New
Orleans as it was in 1845. Norman frequently digresses
on matters that especially concerned him, thus giving
clues to how the many immigrants from the North
viewed New Orleans. As will be further elaborated,
Norman's focus on buildings and other physical features, in addition to his introductory subjects, occasioned many interesting references to the social and
cultural life of the city. The detailed description of
buildings and the numerous accompanying illustrations
are also important sources for a reconstruction of the
architectural history of the period. The general reader
and even the tourist of today, wishing to orient himself

to this history, would do well to begin with an examination of *New Orleans and Environs*.

Besides being historically useful documents, the illustrations in *New Orleans and Environs* contribute significantly to the book's enduring charm. In lieu of photography, a technological curiosity in Norman's time, the reproductions gracing its pages compose some of the earliest visual renderings of the city's points of interest, and many of the illustrations in the book survive as some of the only pictorial evidence of buildings long since destroyed or drastically altered. *New Orleans and Environs*, for example, includes pictures of some twenty-five major structures, of which only eight remain standing.[16] The illustrator, identified in Norman's preface only as "Mr. Cowell," was possibly Joseph Cowell, a scene painter, landscape artist, and son of the renowned English-born artist and actor Joseph Leathly Cowell, if not the famous actor himself.[17] The style of the drawings belongs in the schematic romantic tradition associated with John Constable's landscape painting. The regularized and

---

[16] Based on Samuel J. Wilson, Jr., *Guide to the Architecture of New Orleans, 1699–1959* (New Orleans: Reinhold Publishing Co., 1959), these include (with reference to the page of the illustration in Norman's text): United States Mint (88), St. Louis Cathedral (92), St. Patrick's Church (95), Ursulines Chapel (98), Municipal Hall (127), City Hall or the Cabildo (134), Bank of Louisiana (156), and Merchants' Exchange (161).

[17] Joseph Leathly Cowell (1792–1863), famous English-born actor who spent forty-two years in America, was a portraitist and scene painter as well. His eldest son, Joseph, who died in "early manhood," was also a scene painter. The elder Cowell's daughter made her theatrical debut in New Orleans around 1837 and then settled for a while in St. Louis. The family was certainly familiar with New Orleans, so the artist for Norman's

geometric lines produce a somewhat brittle and flat effect; yet, in keeping with national artistic tastes, the norm followed by Cowell was well suited to the existing appetite for and appreciation of Greek-style monumentalism as *prima facie* evidence of civic progress. Moreover, the flatness of the illustrations nicely complements the cramped size of Norman's volume.[18]

Since an appreciation of the historical significance of *New Orleans and Environs* is enhanced by one's understanding of Norman's era as the Crescent City's Golden Age, some elaboration and qualification of this theme are in order. The eight years Norman had spent in the city before 1845 were, as previously stated, a period of slowed economic development following the crash of 1837. Still, as shown in many construction dates provided by Norman, even those depressed times were characterized by vigorous building and were marked by the only time in the city's history, between 1838 and 1842, when the volume of its export trade exceeded New York's.[19] The 1830s had been years of spectacular growth, and in 1845, fully recovered from the depression, New Orleans looked forward again to what was to be more than a decade of economic boom

---

guidebook could have been either the father or son. Leslie Stephen (ed.), *Dictionary of National Biography* (London: Smith Elder and Co., 1887), XII, 376–77; George C. Groce and David H. Wallace, *The New York Historical Society's Dictionary of Artists in America* (New Haven: Yale University Press, 1957), 151. Professor James H. Dormon of the University of Southwestern Louisiana suggested these possibilities of Cowell's identity.

[18] I am indebted to Professor Gloria K. Fiero of the University of Southwestern Louisiana for her criticism of Cowell's art.

[19] Glaab, *American City*, 68.

extending to the Civil War.[20] Between 1830 and 1840 its population had more than doubled to reach 102,190, passing that of Boston and ranking it as the fourth largest city in the United States, behind New York, Philadelphia, and Baltimore. In 1850 and 1860 the city's population stood at 116,375 and 168,675, respectively, and though by the latter date it had again fallen behind Boston to fifth place, its total increase in the 1850s was exceeded only by that of New York, Philadelphia, and Chicago. A dramatic reversal occurred in the 1860s, for not only did New Orleans drop to eighth place in 1870, surpassed by Chicago, Cincinnati, and St. Louis, but it ranked twentieth in net increment among American cities.[21] During the remainder of the nineteenth century, with the industrial revolution and rapid urbanization taking place in the North, the Crescent City's growth was comparatively slow, and it dropped to twelfth place, with 287,104 inhabitants in 1900, when, according to Norman's prediction, the city's population should have exceeded the million mark. In fact, not until the mid-twentieth century would it attain such numbers, and by then many more American cities had passed New Orleans in population.

[20] John Smith Kendall, *History of New Orleans* (3 vols.; Chicago: Lewis Publishing Co., 1922), I, 143, 160. Kendall's is the standard history of New Orleans in this period.

[21] New Orleans' growth was exceeded by that of Baltimore, Boston, Buffalo, Chicago, Cincinnati, Cleveland, Detroit, Indianapolis, Jersey City, Louisville, Milwaukee, New York, Newark, Philadelphia, Pittsburgh, St. Louis, San Francisco, Scranton, and Washington, D.C. Interestingly, in the twentieth century, New Orleans' total population was to be exceeded by that of thirteen of these cities. See population tables in McKelvey, *American Urbanization*, 37, 73.

The prosperity of New Orleans during the three decades before the Civil War derived from the rapidly
developing agriculture of the Mississippi Valley and the
newly dominant steamboat transportation that turned
increasing amounts of trade from overland to water
routes. The decade of the 1840s was the heyday of the
packet steamers, when adolescents kept abreast of new
speed records on the river as avidly as later generations
of youth would study statistics covering sports heroics.
In 1844 the *J. M. White*'s New Orleans-to-St. Louis
run was just four hours and fifty-six minutes shy of the
celebrated time of the *Robert E. Lee* in 1870, an indica-
tion of how far Norman's "age of steam" did advance in
an area of technology so important to his community.[22]
The port, of course, was the lifeblood of New Orleans,
and the bustling entrepôt attracted a viable influx of
capitalists, mostly of northern origin, including large
numbers of New Yorkers.[23] During the period marked
by rapid expansion of the cotton kingdom in Louisiana
and Texas, New Orleans stood as the Old South's un-
rivaled financial center and slave emporium.[24]

Many optimistic New Orleanians in Norman's life-
time, notably the true believers in the doctrines of
De Bow's Review, adopted the thesis that the Crescent
City's destiny was to serve as the matrix of a great

[22] Harold Sinclair, *The Port of New Orleans* (Garden City, N.Y.:
Doubleday, Doran and Co., 1942), 195–97.
[23] McKelvey, *American Urbanization*, 190.
[24] Sarah Searight, *New Orleans* (New York: Stein and Day, 1973),
88–153; Sinclair, *Port of New Orleans*, 195; Eaton, *Southern Civilization*,
53.

civilization based on human bondage. Such views associated with extreme southern nationalism and slavery expansionism ironically resulted in the Civil War which crippled the economy of the Mississippi Valley and of its principal port. Yet, although the war and its regional consequences retarded later economic growth of New Orleans, other developments of greater long-term significance were already contributing during the antebellum period to the city's relative commercial decline. Indeed, a strong argument has been made that slavery itself inhibited investments in commerce, transportation, and industry and that the ideology of white supremacy informed a way of life and attitudes incompatible with entrepreneurial vigor.[25]

Furthermore, most of the great cities of the future, as time proved, would be centers of manufacturing. But the pace of industrialization, as Norman's brief treatment suggests, was unremarkable in New Orleans and had not been calculated to service distant markets (150–51). And many of Norman's contemporaries recognized in the 1840s and 1850s that canals and railroads were in the process of replacing the Mississippi and other river systems as the principal arteries of American trade. To paraphrase the report of one 1853 observer, the steam engine's significance as a motor for "natural" water transportation, originally contributing as it did to flush times on the riverfronts, was later

[25] Eugene D. Genovese, *The Political Economy of Slavery: Studies in the Economy and Society of the Slave South* (New York: Random House, 1965), 13–36; McKelvey, *American Urbanization*, 18, 34.

more efficiently applied to the railroads' high ground, or to "artificial," channels of commerce. The lower Mississippi Valley's railroad mileage then lagged far behind the upper Middle West's, and Chicago's previously mentioned surge in the 1850s symbolized the commercial emergence of the railroad hub among American cities.[26] Norman contended that for accessibility to all sections of the United States transportation facilities in the environs of New Orleans were "unexcelled." Yet even in 1845 this statement applied with a degree of accuracy only to accessibility by water routes, as were all the routes Norman identified as connecting the Crescent City and points beyond twenty miles away (201–206). Finally, concentration of an impressive sum of money in New Orleans banks masked the fact that native New Orleanians were unable to control the terms of interregional flows of money and merchandise.[27]

Norman devotes minimal space to important political events occurring in the 1840s. Only in reading his description of the Statehouse, for example, is one reminded that under a new state constitution adopted in 1845 the capital was to be removed from the Crescent City. Its destination in Baton Rouge was not then known to Norman (92). A staunch supporter of public education, however, Norman does discuss at some

[26] "Report of Israel D. Andrews on the Trade and Commerce of the British and North American Colonies," 1853, in Glaab, *American City*, 75–77.

[27] Robert C. Reinders, *End of an Era: New Orleans, 1850–1860* (New Orleans: Pelican Publishing Co., 1964), 42–49.

length the contributions in this area made by the three New Orleans municipalities after 1841, and he footnotes the unprecedented decision of the Constitutional Convention of 1845 to provide funds for public instruction and to support the establishment in New Orleans of the University of Louisiana, the predecessor of Tulane University. He also remarks optimistically upon the authorization in 1844 of a new board of health in New Orleans. Yet these tax-supported agencies would provide only meagerly for education during Norman's time (indeed, until the twentieth century), and general acceptance of the public health agency as a forceful regulator awaited lessons of later events, notably a tragic yellow fever epidemic of 1853.[28]

The city existed between 1837 and 1853 as three municipalities, each having its legislative and enforcement functions. The areas of the municipalities had been arranged along ethnic lines with the Latin Creoles largely occupying the First Municipality (the present Vieux Carré), American and Irish immigrants living in the Second Municipality above Canal Street, and a mix of Creoles, Germans, and other foreign immigrants residing in the Third Municipality below Esplanade. A

[28] On public education in New Orleans in the period, consult John P. Dyer, "Education in New Orleans," in Carter, *Past as Prelude*, 126–29. On the public health movement and the creation of a new board of public health in 1846, see Rudolph Matas, *History of Medicine in Louisiana*, ed. John Duffy (2 vols.; Baton Rouge: Louisiana State University Press, 1962), II, 169–72; and on the impact of the yellow fever epidemic of 1853 on the public health movement, John Duffy, *Sword of Pestilence: The New Orleans Yellow Fever Epidemic of 1853* (Baton Rouge: Louisiana State University Press, 1966), 129–45.

single mayor presided over this inefficient troika, and
the most controversial issues of the day were usually
related to the conflicts between Latin Creole and
"American" interests, a rivalry that had originally been
responsible for the division of political jurisdictions.[29]
Beyond the boundaries of the three municipalities in
1845 were such suburbs as Carrollton and Algiers,
mentioned as objects of excursions in Norman's book
and later to be annexed by the city (191–94). Lafayette,
a substantial and fast-growing community mentioned
by Norman (69) as within the city's built-up perimeter
above the Second Municipality, was incorporated by
New Orleans in 1852. Norman notes that the Carrollton
Railroad route traversed a two-mile area of suburban
settlement characterized by "beautiful residences"
(191). This section is today known as the Garden District, bordering St. Charles Avenue and distinguished
by its antebellum mansions.

Norman's guide includes some historically interesting commentary on the Crescent City's heterogeneous
social composition, which invariably intrigued travelers and immigrants. Neat categorization of New Orleanians of the 1840s into groups or classes has resulted
in endless argument, and the complex play of alliances,
mesalliances, and prejudices of this Babylon nearly
defies objective analysis. One approaches the subject
confounded by a seeming infinity of sociological
distinctions—upper and lower class, black and white,

[29] Reinders, *End of an Era*, 51.

slave and free, slave and free person of color, gentleman and quadroon, native and immigrant, immigrant American and immigrant European, native French and immigrant French, Creole and American, and so on. With reference to the middle- and upper-class white man's world of struggle for political and economic dominance, however, the differentiation made between Creole and American has attracted the attention of students as important to an understanding of Norman's society. At variance with a later common usage of the word *Creole*, Norman defines the term in one passage to mean all who were born in New Orleans regardless of parental nativity, though in the following paragraph he excludes those of African descent (73–74).[30] Using Norman's nomenclature, it may be said that by 1845 New Orleans contained a large number of Anglo-Saxon Creoles, or the native-born children of the large number of Americans who had migrated to New Orleans. But since the largest number of Americans had arrived after the Louisiana Purchase of 1803, their children would have been but coming of age in the possession of wealth and power in 1845. The city's principal social conflict in this period, therefore, might be described as one between large groups of immigrant Anglo-Saxon Americans and Latin Creoles.[31]

[30] Other evidence of the view that *Creole* was used to apply to the native born is found in Joseph G. Tregle, Jr., "Early New Orleans Society: A Reappraisal," *Journal of Southern History*, XVIII (February, 1952), 23–24.

[31] Leon Cyprian Soulé, *The Know Nothing Party in New Orleans: A Reappraisal* (Baton Rouge: Louisiana Historical Association, 1961), 5–9.

As befitted the civic-minded role of guidebook author, Norman carefully chose words of praise for the incongruous groups of New Orleans society, excluding by omission the blacks. Most Americans probably did not agree with his statement that temperance, on a par with their exclusiveness, was characteristically a Creole trait (73–74). Many American and English visitors while resenting the standoffishness of Latin Creole society were equally appalled by such apperceived affronts to their puritan standards of morality as pervasive gambling, drunkenness, quadroon balls, and other notorious interracial sexual customs. Above all they were shocked by the Latin belief that the Sabbath should be a day of entertainment. The Americans also faulted the Latin Creoles for their lack of interest in better formal education, apparent hatred of innovation, and civic conservatism. Supporting some of these contentions are Norman's references to the unkempt disorder of the Place d'Armes (later Jackson Square) as compared to the neatness of the American section's Lafayette Square; to the First Municipality's indifference to public schools and street paving; and to the astonishment of the Creoles at the sight of the fine buildings and construction boom in the American section. Norman thus smugly recounts a dialect story of a Latin Creole he knew who, never having left the First Municipality, disdained to believe the reports of grandeur emanating from above Canal Street (65–70, 163–65, 182–83). This "upstart" quality of Second

Municipality boosterism was justified in 1845, for economically the period coincided with American prosperity and Latin Creole stagnation.[32]

The Germans, the Irish, the "nondescript watermen" of American origins (74), and the blacks formed the working-class bedrock of New Orleans in the 1840s. The Germans and Irish were, for the most part, impoverished recent arrivals from the Old World. Having immigrated in great force since the 1820s, by 1850 the city's 11,220 Germans and 20,200 Irish together made up more than a fourth of the population. The Irish clustered in the riverfront sections of the Second Municipality and in the suburb of Lafayette, forming what came to be known as the Irish Channel. The Germans also settled in Lafayette and in the Third Municipality at the other end of town. In comparison to the Irish, relatively more German immigrants had lived in towns, were skilled craftsmen, and entered business. The Irish, peasants who had fled the potato famine, labored commonly at the backbreaking drudgery of digging canals, as they did elsewhere in America. Most of the working-class European immigrants in the 1840s and 1850s continued competing for jobs at the level occupied by blacks.[33]

Persons of African ancestry—18,068 slaves and 9,961 free in 1850—about equaled the combined number of Germans and Irish. The city was remarkable for the

[32] Searight, *New Orleans*, 55, 82.
[33] Reinders, *End of an Era*, 17–20; Charles L. Dufour, "The People of New Orleans," in Carter (ed.), *Past as Prelude*, 37–38.

size, learning, and wealth of its community of free persons of African descent, the majority of whom, nevertheless, worked as craftsmen and domestics. Compared to other cities in the South, it does appear that this class could live tolerably well, and it is not a great exaggeration to remark that the *gens de couleur libres*, more than any other group in proportion to their number, were distinguished in literature. Probably, the relatively more promiscuous Latin Creole society, and urbanity itself, resulted in greater fluidity in race relations in the Crescent City than the more restrictive Anglo-Saxon culture and plantation environment permitted in most of the rest of the Old South. Unfortunately, the sectional crisis and strident defense of slavery during the 1850s brought more rigidity to racial patterns in New Orleans as throughout the South, and many talented free persons of color fled to France.[34]

As to the slaves, many northern and European visitors regarded the institution which held them and the condition of their servility as a blight on the city. With equal justice in hindsight, one must add that the reliable supply of slave sweat figured mightily in the Crescent City's affording the human comforts and cultural refinements for which it was famous. For example, as Frederick Law Olmsted reported in 1853, the famously, or infamously, pleasureable white man's Sunday in New Orleans resulted in plantation slaves dreading being sold down the river to the Crescent City,

[34] Reinders, *End of an Era*, 24–25.

where, they believed, their Sabbath's rest would be denied.[35] Norman's only notable observation about slaves, interestingly enough, appears in relation to their being housed in city prisons, for punishment or for safekeeping in the absence of their owners (130–33).

Norman believed that New Orleans exceeded other American cities in the degree of her generosity to the sick and needy. In crediting responsibility for the many hospitals and asylums, he suggests a commendable output of American and Latin Creole humanitarianism and charity (116–19). The roles of benevolent groups, notably the Young Men's Howard Association (115–16) and the Roman Catholic Church with its religious orders, were most admirable, and Norman justifiably emphasizes the service of the great public Charity Hospital, in which the Sisters of Charity heroically sacrificed. In 1845 the Medical College of Louisiana, as described by Norman (168–69), had recently occupied the site adjacent to Charity Hospital. In exchange for this land grant by the city, its physicians and students serviced the hospital, an arrangement significant in the city's progress in medical and educational research.[36]

As Norman maintained, New Orleans was extraordinary in the United States for the amount of free medical care provided, irrespective of class or nationality, and no city was in greater need, for none could match the grisly death rate of the Crescent City. Of a host of tropical scourges, yellow fever was the greatest and most controversial enemy of human life. Typical of

[35] Henry Arnold Kmen, "The Music of New Orleans," in Carter (ed.), *Past as Prelude*, 226.
[36] Matas, *Medicine in Louisiana*, II, 198–214, 249–50.

commentators of the day, Norman engaged in a bit of theorizing about methods to prevent epidemics, expressing at the same time his bafflement at the conflicting ideas as to the cause of the disease. He recognized a connection, however, between its control and effective sanitation, which he deemed sadly lacking in New Orleans (121–23). Physicians of the day, ignorant of germ theory, disputed endlessly, contending variously that the fever was caused by such sundry miasmic agents as the humid atmosphere, the water, the mud, the sun's rays, and alcoholic spirits. In a city where, Mark Twain once observed, it was possible to walk across the Mississippi River on the backs of mosquitoes, seemingly everything but this pest itself was a subject of suspicion as the causal factor. The belief, cited by Norman, that yellow fever was not contagious was favored by merchants who resisted quarantines of the port. In 1854, following the severe epidemic of the previous year which claimed one-twelfth of the population, the New Orleans Board of Health created a Sanitation Commission and opted for the theory that a chemical reaction between filthy conditions and the humid atmosphere was responsible for the sickness.[37]

The question of the proper cure for yellow fever incurred no less heated disputation than the matter of its cause. Generally, American and Gallic physicians formed two schools in treating the disease. The Americans believed in "heroic" treatment that involved forced vomiting, purgation, sweating, blistering, bloodletting, and prescriptions of massive, poisonous

[37] Duffy, *Sword of Pestilence*, 129–45; Reinders, *End of an Era*, 103–104.

doses of such imagined elixirs as mercury and quinine. Undoubtedly, these well-meaning practitioners killed many more persons than they saved. The Gallic school, on the other hand, reflecting the dominant French practice, prescribed rest and minimal use of drugs on the theory that nature should be left to take its course.[38]

As Norman maintained, New Orleans in 1845 was undistinguished in the United States in its native output of literature and painting. There was no public library, only a limited number of public galleries, and although, as he put it, artists there were, none was worthy of special mention (79–80, 169–72). Such accomplished artists as lived in New Orleans prior to the Civil War were mainly non-native, skilled portraitists whose works adorned the mansions of the rich.[39] In literature the most remarkable development of the time was the publication in the same year as *New Orleans and Environs* of *L'Album*, an anthology of one hundred poems by the distinguished Armand Lanusse and fifteen other native-born *gens de couleur libres*. Otherwise, New Orleans figured in American literature of the antebellum period and later principally as inspiration for talented visitors such as, during Norman's residency, Mark Twain and Walt Whitman.[40]

Commercial pursuits in the Crescent City, Norman believed, took precedence over contemplative and ab-

[38] Duffy, *Sword of Pestilence*, 146–66.

[39] Alberta Collier, "The Art Scene in New Orleans," in Carter (ed.), *Past as Prelude*, 148–49.

[40] Goldstein, "Creative Spirit," in Carter (ed.), *Past as Prelude*, 166–84.

stract forms of artistic expression, but New Orleanians were exceptionally avid in their devotion to theatrical performances, and by the mid-nineteenth century the audiences, especially at the opera, were the most mature in the United States. With their love of balls and pageantry extending back to the early colonial period, the people already possessed a rich musical heritage, including the French opera of the Orleans Theater. Appropriately admired by Norman, its quality was then unsurpassed in the United States. At times before 1845 three opera houses ran simultaneously in New Orleans, and performances at the St. Charles Theater competed with distinction against those of the Orleans Theater. The rebuilt St. Charles, described by Norman as not so grandiose as its fire-ravaged predecessor, was nonetheless one of America's most magnificent theaters (176–79).[41]

For some idea of the possibilities in New Orleans for amusement, or spectacle, beyond the opera, the markets (135–37), racetrack (195), and circus (180), one might dwell on a catalog of violations of the Sabbath prepared on Sunday, March 24, 1844, by Henry Benjamin Whipple, a scandalized northern bishop. In addition to numerous balls, theater engagements, and horseracing, his list included parading, dueling, pugilistic encounters, cockfights, masquerades, waxworks exhibits, magical acts, organ-grinders in the street, open bars, widespread gambling, lakefront excursions, horseback riding, minstrel shows, and dinner

---

[41] Henry A. Kmen, *Music in New Orleans: The Formative Years, 1791–1841* (Baton Rouge: Louisiana State University Press, 1966), 3–200.

parties.[42] New Orleans had obviously earned its reputation, to use today's terminology, as a "fun city." The
annual Mardi Gras had witnessed since 1841 the increasing popularity of the elaborately costumed
Bedouins parade, and guests at city hotels scrambled
for invitations to the balls of the exclusive carnival
krewes.[43] The exquisite *tables d'hôte* of the St. Louis
and St. Charles hotels were spreading appreciation for
Creole cuisine, and in 1840 Antoine Alciatore opened
for business.[44]

Depending on one's esthetic standards, it may be said
that in Norman's period of residency, New Orleans was
in the process either of achieving or of losing architectural distinction. The time was, in either case, marked
by significant building, and some of the descriptions of
public edifices in *New Orleans and Environs* have provided students of architectural history with valuable
sources. A regrettable development in the eyes of some
was the triumph of Greek Revival classicism in the
works of such non-native, formally trained architects as
the brothers Charles B. and James Dakin, James Gallier, and Jacques N. Bussiére dePouilly. The new style
sharply conflicted with French and Spanish provincial
and vernacular lines, which in New Orleans have been
admired for their simplicity and indigenous, innovative
qualities. Also viewed with mixed reactions by critics

---

[42] Eaton, *Southern Civilization*, 144–45.
[43] Laurraine Goreau, "Mardi Gras," in Carter (ed.), *Past as Prelude*,
348.
[44] Phil Johnson, "Good Time Town," in Carter, *Past as Prelude*, 254.

was the appearance of the elaborately laced, cast iron porches, still a characteristic feature of the French Quarter, and the unmortared marble, granite, and brick façades admired by Norman (69), which left newer sections indistinguishable from northern cities.[45] Notwithstanding these disagreements over taste, the Dakins, Gallier, and dePouilly have been praised as masters of their chosen style. Among their famous works completed during the short time of Norman's residence in New Orleans were Dakin's St. Patrick's Church (95), done in the exceptional Gothic; Gallier's and Dakin's Christ Church (99); dePouilly's City Exchange and St. Louis Hotel (157); and Gallier's Municipal Hall (now Gallier Hall, 127–29), under construction in 1845 and later cited by an expert on the form as "one of the most beautiful examples of the smaller Greek Revival public buildings to be found anywhere."[46] Indicative of differing sensibilities, a local student and foe of classicism has dismissed this building as a dry and cold example of the unfortunate vogue.[47]

Well before the 1840s and the building boom of

[45] Nathaniel Cortlandt Curtis, *New Orleans: Its Old Houses, Shops, and Public Buildings* (Philadelphia: J. B. Lippincott, 1933), 129–50; James Marston Fitch, "Creole Architecture, 1718–1860: The Rise and Fall of a Great Tradition," in Carter (ed.), *Past as Prelude*, 71–87; Talbot Hamlin, *Greek Revival Architecture in America: Being an Account of Important Trends in American Architecture and American Life Prior to the War Between the States* (London: Oxford University Press, 1944), 213–33.

[46] Hamlin, *Greek Revival Architecture*, 226.

[47] Fitch, "Creole Architecture," in Carter (ed.), *Past as Prelude*, 85.

Norman's day, the overall physical appearance of New
Orleans had impressed travelers with its extraordinar-
ily urbane quality, as if the city were bigger and older
than it was. The flatness of the surrounding topog-
raphy, the layout of streets, and the proportions of
buildings as well as the crowded dock area and festive
customs of the people undoubtedly explain this
phenomenon. Visitors usually reached the city by
water routes through swamps, and most of them must
have shared Harriet Martineau's reaction in the 1830s
on first viewing the skyline. The buildings, she wrote,
"appeared to stand on flooded lots," and the "churches
seemed to spring out of the water." She was struck too
by the grace and antiquity cast by the Place d'Armes.[48]
The old square, one architectural historian has observed, with its adjacent St. Louis Cathedral, Presby-
tere, and Cabildo (133–34), comprised together with
the adjacent market a remarkable urban plan, unique in
the United States.[49] (Within a few years following the
appearance of *New Orleans and Environs*, the Place
d'Armes, renamed Jackson Square, would acquire its
quite different present-day aspect with the erection of
the equestrian monument, overshadowing cathedral
steeples, and the flanking Pontalba apartments.)
Britishers James Logan and Charles Joseph Latrobe in
the 1830s commented on the handsomeness of the city's

[48] *Retrospect of Western Travel* (2 vols.; New York: Harper and
Brothers, 1838), I, 258, 268.
[49] Hamlin, *Greek Revival Architecture*, 214–15. Norman identifies the
latter two as the Court House and City Hall of the First Municipality.

buildings, the colored stuccoes, the iron balconies, the paved streets, and the spaciousness of the latter in the American section with its border on Canal Street.[50] By 1845 Thomas Low Nichols from New Hampshire found astonishing the "massive and magnificent buildings" and the extraordinary number of fine hotels, theaters, exchanges, and banking houses.[51]

Contributing to many a visitor's sense of the Crescent City's importance were the truly marvelous St. Charles and St. Louis hotels, justifiably given prominent mention in Norman's text (137–43, 157–59). One English rambler in New Orleans in 1846, Alexander Mackay, claimed that while the city's public buildings were "neither elegant nor imposing," the St. Charles Hotel was magnificent and unmatched by any hotel in Europe. He contended that in England hotels were small and regarded highly for their intimacy, as one regards "personal property," whereas in America, hotels assumed "the character of public buildings."[52] Indeed, the St. Charles and dePouilly's more architecturally remarkable St. Louis Hotel set examples for other cities to fashion their hostelries on multipurpose and monumental scales. More than a shelter for weary transients, these grand new American hotels dazzled

[50] James Logan, *Notes of a Journey Through Canada, the United States of America, and the West Indies* (Edinburgh: Fraser and Co., 1838), 178; Charles J. Latrobe, *The Rambler in North America* (2 vols.; London: R. B. Seeley and W. Burnside, 1836), II, 330.

[51] Thomas Low Nichols, *Forty Years of American Life, 1821–1861* (New York: Stockpole Sons, 1937), 126.

[52] Cited in Boorstin, *National Experience*, 135.

the guest with elegantly appointed meeting halls, dining and ball rooms, lobbies, and bars. The spirit of this new genre was nowhere in America more masterfully surmounted than by the brilliantly executed dome above the rotunda of the City Exchange and St. Louis Hotel. Without reference to the intrinsic esthetic merits of its classical design, the French-born dePouilly's work was a striking edifice in the city of *New Orleans and Environs*. Its classicism was more generalized and less rigid than that of other local specimens, and was confined to interior appearance so that the façade did not conflict with the French Quarter ambience. Its artful dome, imaginatively enforced with hollow pots, a little-known Renaissance technique, was suited to community values modeled on ancient grandeur.[53]

Norman's section on "The Olden Times" (184–89) will be read by today's Crescent City preservationist with anguish and distress, not only because of the realization that Norman's plea to save the Old Spanish Building and the Bienville House proved futile, but also because of the recognition that the great majority of the buildings he described, resplendent in their time, have long since vanished. Reflecting on a city enraptured in 1975 by the opening of a giant domed multipurpose facility, the glorious domes of the St. Charles and St. Louis Hotels, and their fates, readily come to mind—the former destroyed by fire, the latter tragically de-

[53] Curtis, *New Orleans*, 174–86.

molished in 1915 after years of serving primarily as a delapidated habitat for bats. Although town and suburban houses surviving since 1845 make up a substantial list, probably fewer than twenty of the public buildings described by Norman as existent or projected are substantially intact today.[54]

It should be emphasized, finally, that the Crescent City of 1845 was for many Americans an important symbol of the United States' triumphant nationalism. An event occurring within the memory of the older generation of that day, the Louisiana Purchase, the exemplar of Manifest Destiny, was occasioned by the urgency of acquiring the Mississippi River port. A nearly disastrous second contest for American independence, the War of 1812, was remembered mainly as an image of American invincibility in the Battle of New Orleans, which Norman, in the patriotic fashion of the period, discusses at the conclusion of his work (196–200). In addition to its symbolic significance, New Orleans was also an early example of the paradoxical development of an American nationalism at once imposing cultural assimilation and conformity, and building upon cultural diversity and individuality. In no city in the United States at any time in the history of the country did these contradictory elements produce a more colorful and historically engaging social milieu

[54] In addition to those listed in note 16 above, buildings identified in Wilson's *Guide to Architecture* include part of the United States Barracks (86–87), St. Augustine's Church (96), Mortuary Chapel (97), Ursuline Row Houses (103–104), and Louisiana State Bank (153).

than the New Orleans of the 1840s with its mixture of
English aristocratic, American, and Creole values.
New Orleans and Environs provides much evidence
that Norman, proud New Yorker though he was, embraced this diversity enthusiastically, for the fact of
difference, as well as the city's commercial prominence,
made his subject fascinating. Thus, republication of
Norman's guide with its blending of nationalism, urban
boosterism, description of cultural distinctiveness,
faith in the future, and respect for the past seems a
fitting memorial in the complex age of the United
States bicentennial observance.

NORMAN'S NEW ORLEANS
AND ENVIRONS

NEW ORLEANS.

NORMAN'S

NEW ORLEANS AND ENVIRONS:

CONTAINING A BRIEF HISTORICAL SKETCH

OF THE

TERRITORY AND STATE OF LOUISIANA,

AND THE

CITY OF NEW ORLEANS,

FROM THE EARLIEST PERIOD TO THE PRESENT TIME:

PRESENTING

A COMPLETE GUIDE

TO ALL SUBJECTS OF GENERAL INTEREST IN THE SOUTHERN
METROPOLIS;

WITH A

CORRECT AND IMPROVED PLAN OF THE CITY, PICTORIAL ILLUSTRA-
TIONS OF PUBLIC BUILDINGS, ETC.

NEW ORLEANS:
PUBLISHED BY B. M. NORMAN.
NEW YORK, D. APPLETON & CO.; PHILADELPHIA, GEO. S. APPLETON;
BOSTON, JAS. MUNROE & CO.; CINCINNATI, H. W. DERBY & CO.;
ST. LOUIS, HALSALL & COLLET; MOBILE, J. M. SUMWALT & CO.

1845.

Wm. Van Norden, Printer, 39 William street.

DEDICATED

TO THE

CITIZENS OF NEW ORLEANS,

WITH

True Sentiments of Respect,

BY THEIR

HUMBLE SERVANT,

The Publisher.

NEW ORLEANS, October, 1845.

PREFACE.

To the stranger visiting New Orleans, and to those abroad who may feel an interest in the metropolis of the great South-West, no apology may be urged for the present work. Curiosity, in the one case, and necessity, in the other, will prove a sufficient plea, and prepare the way for that favorable reception, which it has been the aim of the publisher it should deserve. And, judging from the interest he has taken in compiling it, he flatters himself it will be found a communicative and agreeable companion to both the above classes of readers, and to the public in general.

The tables and index have been prepared with great care, and will be found highly convenient to those who wish to consult the work with reference to any particular subject of which it treats. All such subjects are there so arranged and classified, that the reader may see, at a glance, where they are to be found.

The engravings were executed by Messrs. Shields & Hammond, after original drawings, made expressly for this work, by Mr. Cowell. The plan of the city was engraved by the same artists, after an original draught by Mr. Mull-hausen.

To several gentlemen, who have kindly aided the publisher in gathering materials for the work, he would here express his grateful acknowledgements.   For the historical
facts embodied in the volume, he is indebted to several
works on the history of Louisiana, and the discovery and
early settlement of our country.

NORMAN'S

NEW ORLEANS AND ENVIRONS.

—

A BRIEF SKETCH OF THE DISCOVERY AND TERRITORIAL HISTORY OF LOUISIANA.

TOMOWEN. *PINXT.*
De Soto's discovery of the Mississippi.

—

LOUISIÁNA is the name given by the French, to all that extensive tract of land, lying West of the Mississippi River, which was ceded by them to the United States in 1803. The line of its western boundary follows the Sabine River to the 32d degree of north latitude ; thence, due north to the

Red River; along that stream westerly to the meridian of 100 west longitude; thence due north to the Arkansas River, ascending that to its source; thence due north to the 42d degree of latitude; and along that, parallel to the Pacific Ocean. Its northern boundary is a matter of dispute between the United States and Great Britain, and the discussion, at the present moment is somewhat exciting and ominous. It is the only question in relation to any part of our border, which has not been amicably adjusted by treaty. *We* claim the boundary formed by a line drawn from the Lake of the Woods, in the 49th degree of latitude, due west to the Rocky Mountains, thence to the parallel of 54, and on that to the Pacific. The British, on the other hand, claim that part, lying west of the Rocky Mountains, and north of the 46th parallel, or the latitude of the Columbia River. Our claim to the whole of this Territory, the part in dispute being called the Oregon, is based upon priority of discovery, and purchase. The British claim the northern portion by right of possession. The question has been held in suspense for several years, under a treaty of joint occupancy, which is now about to terminate. The question of ownership and jurisdiction, will probably be adjusted definitely in the course of a few years. We trust it may be done without the necessity of an appeal to arms.

The vast domain, included within the above named boundaries, contains more than twelve hundred thousand square miles. It is about six times the size of France, and nearly twice as large as the whole territory embraced in the thirteen original States of the Union—an empire, in itself sufficiently extensive to satisfy the ambition of any ordinary people.

The discoveries of Columbus, and his immediate successors, were confined to the islands in and about the Gulf of Mexico, and a part of the adjacent coast of the two Continents. The immense tracts that lay inland, stretching thousands of miles towards the setting sun, were unknown and unexplored for nearly half a century after the landing of the Europeans on this coast. Those of North America were first visited in 1512, by Juan Ponce de Leon, a Spanish adventurer in quest of the FOUNTAIN OF IMMORTAL YOUTH, which the Indians represented as gushing up in one of the Elysian Valleys of the West;—but, unfortunately for him and for posterity, death overtook him before he reached the *Fountain*, and the directions for finding it perished with him. Having made the first land on Pascha *Florida*, or Palm Sunday, he gave the name of Florida to all the country lying to the North and West.

In consequence of the premature death of Ponce de Leon, the expedition was given up, and little

1*

more was known of these regions until 1538, when Hernandez de Soto, having been made Governor of Cuba, and Adelantado of Florida, undertook, with a company of six hundred men, to explore these his western dominions. He penetrated Florida, Georgia, Tennessee and Kentucky, and struck the Mississippi not far from the place now known as the Chickasaw Bluffs. Thence he passed over to the Red River, and descending that, had nearly reached its mouth, when he was seized with a sudden fever, and died. To prevent his body from falling into the hands of the Indians, it was sunk in the stream at the mouth of Red River, near its junction with " *the father of waters.*"

The expedition of de Soto consumed four years, during which, his adventures, among the various tribes and nations then teeming in these quiet regions, were diversified and full of the most romantic interest. He was succeeded in 1542 by Lewis de Moscoso, or Mucoso, who, with none of the address or enterprise of de Soto, found himself and his small company, now reduced by disease and constant warfare with the natives, to about three hundred men, encompassed with difficulty, and in danger of being entirely cut off. They built seven brigantines, probably the first specimens of scientific ship building on the Mississippi, and then dropped down the river. Pursued by thousands of exasperated Indians in their canoes, harrassed, wounded, and some of them slain, the miserable remnant at length found their way out of the river, about the middle of July.

No sooner had they put to sea, than a violent tempest arose; when another calamity befel them, which will be feelingly understood by many of the navigators of these waters, in our own day. I will give it in the language of the historian, who was one of the party. "While they were in this tempest, in great fear of being cast away, they endured an intolerable torment of an infinite swarm of musketoes, which fell upon them, which, as soon as they had stung the flesh, it so infected it, as though they had been venomous. In the morning, the sea was assuaged, and the wind slacked, but not the musketoes; for the sails, which were white, seemed black with them in the morning. Those which rowed, unless others kept them away, were not able to row. Having passed the fear and danger of the storm, beholding the deformities of their faces, and the blows which they gave themselves to drive them away, one of them laughed at another."

It is manifest from the narrative of de Soto's expedition, that a dense population once covered this whole territory. It is equally manifest that they were a race infinitely superior to the almost exterminated tribes which still remain. In the

arts of what we term civilization, in the comforts
and conveniences of social life, in the organization of society, in works of taste, in a knowledge
of the principles, and an appreciation of the beauties
of architecture, and in the application of the various mechanical powers requisite to the construction of buildings on a grand and magnificent scale,
they may challenge comparison with some of the
proudest nations of antiquity, in the old world.
What has become of those mysterious nations, we
are at a loss to conjecture; but their works remain, though in ruins, eternal monuments of their
genius and power.   As far as they have been
explored, they afford ample evidence that the
appellation " New World" is an entire misnomer.
As the eloquent Mr. Wirt once said—" *This is the
old World*," and the day may come, when the
antiquarian will find as much that is attractive
and interesting in the time hallowed ruins and the
almost buried cities, of America, as those of Pom-
peii and Herculaneum, of Thebes and Palmyra.

Changed as the whole country has been, in the
lapse of three centuries, in respect to most of
those things which must have struck the original
discoverers with wonder, admiration, and awe—
there is one feature, as described by de Soto, that
still remains, so distinct and characteristic, that,
if the brave old Adelantado should suddenly rise

from his watery grave, he would immediately re-cognize the place of his burial.

The Mississippi is still the same as when those bold adventurers first beheld it. The historian describes it as "a river so broad, that if a man stood still on the other side, it could not be dis-cerned whether he was a man or no. The chan-nel was very deep, the current strong, the water muddy and filled with floating trees."

Of all the great rivers of this continent, it is a distinction which is probably peculiar to the Mis-sissippi, that it was discovered, not by navigators entering it from the ocean, but by a band of ad-venturous explorers, striking it in their march, at some thousand miles from its mouth!

For more than a century after the expedition of de Soto, these mighty regions were suffered to remain in the quiet possession of their original owners, undisturbed by the visits of white men. In 1654, the adventurous Col. Woods, from the infant colony of Virginia, wandered into these then remote regions, and crossed "the great river," after which it lay forgotten for twenty years longer.

In 1673, Marquette, a French monk, and Joliet, a trader, starting from Quebec, traversed the great northern Lakes, ascended the Fox River to its source, made a small portage west to the Wiscon-sin, and descended that river to the Mississippi, where they arrived on the 7th of July. Committing themselves to the current, the two solitary travellers reached a village of the Illinois, near the mouth of the Missouri, where they were kindly received and hospitably entertained. After a brief stay, they proceeded down to a settlement of the Arkansas, near the river of that name. They did not proceed farther at this time, but returned to Quebec, by the same route, fully impressed with the belief that they could reach the Gulf of Mexico, by continuing their course on the great river. There was immense rejoicing in Quebec at the result of this adventure. *Te deum* was sung in the Churches, on the occasion, and the great Western Valley set down as belonging to France by right of discovery. They were little aware how brief their dominion in that land would be, or how soon the fruits of all their toils would fall into the hands of a nation then unborn, that in one little century, should leap to independence and power, and claim an honorable place among the hoary empires of the earth.

Six years after the return of Marquette and Joliet, Robert, Chevalier de la Salle, commenced operations for a further exploration of the Mississippi. With seventeen men, he proceeded to the Little Miami, near the mouth of which he built a fort. From thence he traversed the country, till he came to the Falls of St. Anthony. Descending the Mississippi to the Gulf of Mexico, he returned by land to Quebec during the year 1681. He then proceeded to France, procured a vessel, and sailed in 1685, with the intention of entering the river through the Gulf, but was unable to find its mouth.

In his next voyage, having met with the same disappointment, he erected a fort in the Bay of St. Bernard, near the mouth of the Colorado. Ascending that river, about sixteen miles, he established another fort, which, however, he soon destroyed, and returned to the first settlement. Here he built houses, erected another fort, which he called St. Louis, and prepared the ground for cultivation. He made many abortive attempts to find the entrance to the Mississippi. At length, a conspiracy was formed among his own party, and he was cruelly murdered by Dehault, on the 19th of March, 1687, near the western branch of Trinity River. Thus fell, in the midst of his toils, and in the prime of his years, by the hand of an assassin, one of the most renowned adventurers of the 17th century—a man who may be justly claimed as an honor to the country that gave him birth. He deserved a better fate. In cool courage, in hardy enterprise, and in fertility of resources, he was second only to Columbus. And in the power of subduing the wild spirits of his men, and bending all their energies to the one object

before him, he displayed much of the sagacity and
tact of that great navigator. In vigor, decision
and promptitude, he much resembled the renowned
Cortes, without any of the bigotry or cruelty, that
tarnished the reputation of the Conqueror of
Mexico.

In 1699, eighteen years after La Salle had demonstrated the connection of the Mississippi with the
Gulf of Mexico, by passing out at its mouth, Iberville succeeded in entering it from the Gulf.
Ascending as far as the junction of Red River,
he returned, and proceeded, by way of the Gulf,
into Lake Pontchartrain. He formed a settlement
and erected a fort, at Biloxi, which he left under
the command of his brother Bienville, while he returned to France, to induce others to join the colony.
Soon after he left, the new commander ascended
the Mississippi as far as the present site of New
Orleans. In returning, he met a British vessel of
sixteen guns, under the command of Capt. Bard,
who enquired the bearings of the great river, inti-
mating that it was his intention to establish a colony
upon its banks. Bienville, in reply, directed him
to go farther west, and thus induced him to turn
about; from which circumstance, the place of
their meeting was called " The English Turn," a
name which it retains to this day.

Iberville accompanied by a considerable accession of force, comprising hardy settlers, and

scientific men, soon returned to the colony. Finding things in a promising condition, he proceeded up the river as far as Natchez, and planted a settlement there. Leaving Bienville and St. Denys in command, he again took leave, and sailed for France. He was indefatigable in his exertions to establish and render permanent his little colony. It was the first attempt in this section ; and Iberville may be well regarded as the father of Louisiana. But he did not survive to enjoy its growth and prosperity. He died in one of the West India Islands, a victim to the yellow fever, in 1708. About this time, one Sauville was elected Governor. He survived the appointment, however, but a short time. Bienville then succeeded him, and retained the office till 1710, when he was superseded by De Muys and Diron d'Artaquette.

Finding that they derived no immediate advantage from this new accession of territory, the French Government, in 1712, granted to Antonio Crozat, a rich merchant of Paris, the monopoly of the trade of Louisiana, which he surrendered back in 1717. What a fortune a man might make now, out of a five years monopoly of the trade of that luxuriant region !

In 1717, a new charter was issued, under the style of " The Western Company," with the exclusive privilege of the trade of Louisiana for twenty-five years. Bienville was again chosen Governor, and in the following year, 1718, he laid the foundation of New Orleans. Hitherto the pursuits of agriculture had been entirely neglected. Whether this neglect was attributable to the hostility of the Indians, compelling them to concentrate their little force in one spot, or to the flattering promises of trade, or to the illusive hope of discovering mines of gold, which occupied all their time, or to all these causes combined, we cannot now determine. We only know, that, up to this period, they had depended almost entirely upon supplies sent from France, for the common necessaries of life. But now, the cultivation of the soil begun to be an object of considerable attention, tobacco and rice being the principal articles from which a profit was expected.

The chief personage in this "Western Company," was the notorious John Law, a Scotch financier, one of those universal speculators, who experiment upon every thing, human and divine, who revel only in change, and to whom mere innovation becomes the professional business of a life. As is usual in such cases, he managed so as to draw down ruin upon himself and his duped associates in France, while at the same time, he had the singular tact to place the colony in a condition for the time. The result of his schemes, however, was ultimately disastrous. The finances of the colony were thrown into inextricable confusion. The French Ministry, instead of applying an efficient remedy, or leaving the evil to cure itself, only tampered with it, by changing the values of the coins, and thus deranging all the money transactions of the colony. The effect was ruinous to some, and embarrassing to all. And when was it otherwise? Never. History and experience utter but one voice on the subject of governmental experiments, and arbitrary legislative innovations, upon ordinary fiscal operations, and the course of trade. And that voice is— *"hands off."*

In the mean time war was declared between France and Spain. The colonists, sympathizing with the mother country, commenced offensive operations against their neighbors in Florida, and took possession of Pensacola; which, however, the Spaniards soon recovered. The trade of war was never very profitable, even to conquerors. No sooner were the different colonies of pale faces at loggerheads among themselves, than their natural enemies, the Indians, began to take advantage of their divisions, and to endeavor to exterminate them both. A horrible massacre took place at Natchez, in 1729. This was but part of a plan which had been formed among the Mississippi tribes, for a general butchery throughout the colony. The Natchez tribe, mistaking the day appointed for the sacrifice, commenced their work of blood too soon, and thus gave timely warning of the plot to all the other settlements. The war which followed was a destructive one, but the Indians were ultimately defeated.

Bienville, having returned to France in 1727, was succeeded by Perrier. Under his administration, the agricultural enterprise of the colony was considerably advanced. The cultivation of indigo was commenced in 1728. The fig tree and the orange were introduced at the same time.

In 1732, ten years before the legal expiration of their monopoly, the "Western Company" returned their charter to the King. The colony was then scarcely more than thirty years old, yet, notwithstanding their many and severe trials, by war and by disease, the population numbered five thousand whites, and two thousand blacks. Bienville was, the third time, appointed Governor, having the entire confidence both of the government and of the people. He continued to exercise this office till 1741, when he again resigned, carrying with him into private life the regrets and affectionate regards of the inhabitants. He was succeeded by the Marquis de Vandreuil.

In the winter of 1747–8, the orange plantations were visited by a severe frost, such as had never been known before, which not only cut off the crop for the season, but almost destroyed the prospects of that branch of business in the colony.

The cultivation of the sugar cane, now so extensive and lucrative a branch of business, did not begin to attract the attention of agriculturalists till 1751. It was then introduced by the Jesuits of St. Domingo, who sent some of the plants, as a present to their brethren in Louisiana, accompanied by negroes, well acquainted with its cultivation, and with the process then in use for manufacturing it into sugar. The lower part of the Fauxbourg of St. Mary was devoted to this experiment. That it was a happy experiment for the colony, and the country, the waving fields and princely estates on every side, and the annually increasing supply of this great staple, bear ample witness.

A large accession was made to the population of the colony in 1754, by the arrival of emigrants from Acadia, (Nova Scotia) which they were compelled to leave, owing to the oppresssive measures of the British Government, by which that province had just been conquered. A few years afterwards, great numbers of Canadians, fleeing from the same oppressions, found refuge in the sunny vallies of the south, and brought a very considerable acquisition of strength and wealth to the colony.

" The seven years' war" between France and England, ended in the cession, to the latter power, of all the French possessions in North America, except Louisiana. It was stipulated, between the two crowns, that the boundary line of their respective dominions, in the New World, should run along the middle of the Mississippi, from its source as far as the Iberville, and along the middle of that river, and of Lakes Maurepas and Ponchartrain. This was in 1763. In the course of the same year, Louisiana was transferred by treaty to the crown of Spain. The tidings of this unexpected cession, which were not promulgated until two years after the execution of the treaty, spread dismay through the colony. The idea of being passed over, *nolens volens*, to the domination of Spaniards, was revolting to the thousands of true hearted and loyal Frenchmen, who had acquired and defended the territory, and claimed it as their own. They resolved, as one man, to resist this unceremonious change of masters, apparently determined, if their old mother, France, persisted in casting them off, to set up for themselves.

In pursuance of this resolution, they refused to receive Don Ulloa, whom the King of Spain despatched in 1766, to take possession of the Province, and to assume the Government, as his representative. The point was disputed at the cannon's mouth, but the colony prevailed, and Don Ulloa returned with his dishonored commission, to his master. Charles was as indignant as his crest-fallen servant, at this unexpected repulse.

But he was too busy with his own troubles at home, to pursue the matter at that moment.

A fit instrument of Royal vengeance was at length found, in the person of Don O'Reilley, a renegade Irishman, who, in 1769, was appointed to subdue and rule over the refractory province. A more perfect exemplification of the remark, that the most depraved unprincipled man may gain the confidence and regard of Kings, can scarcely be found. In the execution of his trust, he showed himself a very fiend incarnate. First, by fair promises, cautiously mingled with just as much of intimidation, as would give an air of candor and courtly conciliation to his promises, he induced the too credulous Louisianians to abandon their purpose of resistance, and surrender without striking a blow. This artful guise he continued to wear, till he had obtained possession of all the insignia of government, and the sinews of power, and placed his own chosen tools in all the chief places of trust. Then the mask of hypocrisy was boldly thrown off, and the cloven foot uncovered. His fair promises were immediately shown to be only a master stroke of policy, to gain an end. In the face of his solemn stipulations, he caused those who had been foremost in refusing submission to his authority, to be seized and put to death. Five of them, principal citizens of New Orleans, he caused to be publicly shot. Five more he consigned to the dungeons of the Moro, at Havana, and one he procured to be assassinated. Other acts of cold-blooded cruelty, and false-hearted tyranny followed, till he became the execration and abhorrence of the whole colony. He introduced the Spanish colonial system, and subjected the inhabitants to every species of indignity and abuse. At length, the extravagance of his measures, and his unprincipled abuse of power, wrought its own ruin. He was recalled by his King, and disgraced—if one already so infamous could by any means be rendered more so. His successor was Unzoga, who was shortly after superseded by Galvez.

The colony now enjoyed a brief season of comparative quiet. But the war between England and Spain, which broke out in 1779, afforded an opportunity for Governor Galvez to show his loyal zeal, and exercise his military talents. With the troops under his command, he invaded Florida, took possession of Baton Rouge, and Fort Charlotte, near Mobile, and proceeded to Pensacola, which, after an obstinate resistance, also submitted to his authority. Thus was the Spanish dominion completely established in Florida.

Governor Miro, who succeeded Galvez, carried into full effect the colonial system of Spain, which was by no means relished by the French inhabitants of the colony.

In 1785, a new firebrand was thrown into the

midst of these combustible elements. An attempt was made to establish an office of the Inquisition in Louisiana. It was fearlessly opposed, and fortunately crushed without bloodshed. The agent, to whom the obnoxious business was entrusted, was seized in his bed, conveyed forcibly on board a vessel, and sent home to Spain.

A census of the province, taken in 1788, just ninety years from the date of the first settlement, showed a population of 42,611. Of these, 19,445 were whites, 21,465 slaves, and 1701 colored freemen. New Orleans, then 70 years old, contained 5,338 inhabitants.

The Baron de Carondelet was appointed Governor in 1792. During his administration, in the year 1794, the first newspaper, called " Le Moniteur," was published in Louisiana. At the same period the Canal Carondelet was commenced; and the cultivation of indigo and the sugar cane, which had hitherto been the great staples of the colony, was suspended.

In 1795, by the treaty of St. Lorenzo, the navigation of the Mississippi was opened to the western States of the Union, and the great impulse given to the commercial prosperity of New Orleans, which secured forever the pre-eminence of the Crescent City. The same treaty defined the boundaries, as they now exist, between Florida and Mississippi. But Carondelet, being rather

2

more tardy in yielding possession, than suited the active, enterprizing spirit of the Americans, the territory was seized by an armed force, under Andrew Elliott.

Two years after this, a plan set on foot by Carondelet, to dismember the American Union, by drawing the Western States into a separate compact, was detected and defeated by the address of General Wilkinson. Whether Aaron Burr was in the plot, or only took a hint from it a few years later, does not appear of record. Carondelet was succeeded by Gayosa de Lamor, Casa Calvo, and Salvado, who, successively, but for a very brief period, wielded the chief magistracy of the colony.

In 1803, Louisiana was re-transferred to France, and immediately sold to the United States for 15,000,000 of dollars. The treaty which accomplished this important object was entered into on the 30th of April. Possession was taken, in behalf of the United States, by General Wilkinson and William C Claiborne, amid the rejoicings of a people attached to liberty, and eager to grasp at any opportunity to shake off the yoke of Spain.

The population of Louisiana, at the time of the purchase, did not exceed fifty thousand, exclusive of the Indians, and these were scattered over every part of its immense territory. Seven years after, the population had nearly trebled, and her prosperity had advanced in equal proportion.

The year 1812 was a memorable era in the history of Louisiana, and marked with incidents never to be forgotten by her citizens. It was in this year, that the first Steam Boat was seen on the bosom of " the great river," now alive with hundreds of these winged messengers, plying to and fro. In the same year war was declared with Great Britain, and Louisiana, as now constituted, was admitted, as an independent State, into the great American Confederacy.

THE STATE OF LOUISIANA.

Plantation House and Works.

THE State of Louisiana is bounded on the north by the states of Arkansas, and Mississippi; on the east by the latter and the Gulf of Mexico; on the south by the Gulf of Mexico, and on the west by Mexico and Texas. It is a well watered garden, the soil being rich, and intersected by the Mississippi, Red, and Wachita Rivers, and many inferior streams, and washed, on its western limit, by the Sabine.

The face of the country is exceedingly level, so much so, that in a portion equal to three fourths of the State, there is scarcely a hill to be found. Those parts that are covered with pine woods are usually uneven, sometimes rising into fine swells, with broad table summits, intersected with valleys from thirty to forty feet deep. They do not lie in any particular range, but, like the ocean in a high and regular swell, present a uniform undulated surface. The alluvial soil is, of course level, and the swamps, which are only inundated alluvions, are dead flats.

A range of gentle elevations commences in Opelousas, and gradually increasing in height as it advances, diverges toward the Sabine. In the vicinity of Natchitoches, this range holds its way northwestwardly; about half way between the Red and the Sabine Rivers, and continues to increase in altitude, till it reaches the western border of the State. Seen from the pine hills above Natchitoches, it has the blue outline and general aspect of a range of mountains.

Another line of hills, commencing not far from Alexandria, on the northern side of the Red River, and separating the waters of that stream from those of the Dudgemony, extends northwardly, till it approaches, and runs into, the mammillæ, or bluffs, that bound the alluvions of the Wachita, diverging gradually from the line of that stream, as it passes beyond the western limits of the State.

That remote part of Natchitoches called Allen's

settlement, is a high rolling country. There are also hills of considerable magnitude on the east side of the Mississippi, beyond the alluvions. But generally speaking, Louisiana may be considered as one immense plain, divided into pine woods, prairies, alluvions, swamps, and hickory and oak lands.

The pine-wood lands, as I have already said, are usually rolling. There are some exceptions, but they are very few. They have almost invariably a poor soil. Some of those west of Opelousas, and those between the Wachita and Red Rivers, are even sterile, answering well to the name by which they are called in some other parts of the country, Pine Barrens.

Some parts of the prairies of Opelousas are of great fertility, and those of Attakapas are still more so. As a general feature, they are more level than those of the upper country. An extensive belt of these prairies, bordering on the Gulf of Mexico, is low and marshy, and subject to be wholly inundated in any extraordinary swell of the river. A considerable portion of them have a cold clayey soil, the surface of which, under the influence of a warm sun, hardens into a stiff crust. In other portions, the soil is of an inky blackness, and often, in the hot and dry season, cracks in long fissures some inches in width.

The bottoms are generally rich, but in very

different degrees. Those of the Mississippi and Red Rivers, and the bayous connected with these streams, are more fertile than those on the western border of the State. The quality of the richer bottoms of the Mississippi, as well as those of the Red River, is sufficiently attested by the prodigious growth of timber in those parts, the luxuriance of the cane and the cotton, the tangles of vines and creepers, the astonishing size of the weeds—which, however, find it difficult to over-top the better products of the soil—and the universal strength of the vegetation.

The most productive district of this State, is a belt of land, called "*the Coast,*" lying along the Mississippi, in the neighborhood of New Orleans. It consists of that part of the bottom, or alluvion, of the Great River, which commences with the first cultivation above the Balize, about forty miles below the capital, and extends about one hundred and fifty miles above it. This belt on each side of the river, is secured from an overflow by an embankment, called "*the levee,*" from six to eight feet in height, and sufficiently broad, for the most part, to furnish an excellent highway. The river, in an ordinary rise, would cover the greater part of these beautiful bottoms, to a depth of from two to six feet, if they were not thus protected. This belt is from one to two miles in width; a richer tract of land, of the same extent, cannot probably be found on the face of the globe.

On the east side of the river the levee extends to Baton Rouge, where it meets the highlands ; on the west side, it continues, with little interruption, to the Arkansas line. On the east, above the levee, are the parishes of Baton Rogue and West Feliciana. This latter received its appropriate and expressive name from its beautifully variegated surface of fertile hills and valleys, and its rare combination of all the qualities that are most to be desired in a planting country. It is a region of almost fairy beauty and wealth. The soil literally teems with the most luxuriant productions of this favored clime. The hills are covered with laurel, and forest trees of magnificent growth and foliage, indicating a soil of the richest and most productive character. Here are some of the wealthiest and most intelligent planters, and the finest plantations in the state, the region of princely taste and luxury, and more than patriarchal hospitality. The mouth of Bayou Sara, which is the point of shipment for this productive region, transmits immense quantities of cotton to New Orleans. Some of the plantations on this bayou have from five to eight hundred acres under cultivation.

On the western side of the Mississippi, are the Bayous Lafourche and Plaquemine, outlets, or arms of the Great River, and subject, of course, to all its fluctuations. The bottoms bordering on these bayous are of the same luxuriant soil, as those on the parent stream, and are guarded from inundation in the same manner, by levees. In this region, the sugar cane is exceedingly productive. It is estimated that, within a compass of seven miles from Thibadeauxville, in the vicinity of the Bayous Black and Terre Bonne, about one tenth of the sugar crop of Louisiana is produced.

A considerable part of Attakapas is also very productive, as well as portions of Opelousas. The latter, however, is better adapted to grazing. The Teche, which meanders through the former, and the eastern part of the latter, of these two parishes, never overflows its banks. The land rises from the river, in a regularly inclined plane towards the woods, affording free courses for the streams, which discharge themselves into the bayou. The soil, therefore, cannot be called alluvial, though in the most essential quality of productiveness, it is scarcely inferior to the best of them. It is a lovely region, the most beautiful, perhaps, in the whole Union, for agricultural purposes. But it has one great drawback, especially for the cultivation of sugar; there is a deficiency of ordinary fire-wood; though the live-oak abounds there to such an extent, that Judge Porter once remarked in Congress, that " there was enough of it in At-

2*

takapas, to supply the navies of the whole world with ship timber."

The lands on the Atchafalaya are of an excellent quality, and would afford a desirable opening for enterprising cultivators, if they were not liable to frequent inundations, an evil which will doubtless be remedied, as the population and wealth of that section advances. Those on the Courtableau, which runs through Opelousas, are equal in point of fertility, to any in that parish. From thence, proceeding northward, by Bayou Bœuf, we find, on that bayou, a soil which is regarded by many as the best in the State for the cultivation of cotton. There is also land of an excellent quality on bayou Rouge, though it is, as yet, for the most part, in the state of nature. The banks of the Bayou Robert, still further north, are of extraordinary fertility, the cane brake, a sure evidence of a very rich soil, flourishing with astonishing luxuriance. Bayou Rapid, which gives its name to the parish through which it runs, intersects one of the most beautiful tracts in the state, which is laid out, on both sides of the bayou, through the whole length of its course, into the finest cotton plantations.

The bottoms of the Red River are well known for their fertility. Those which lie about its lower courses are justly esteemed the paradise of cotton planters. The soil is of a darkish red color, occasioned by the presence of the red oxide of iron. It is thought to derive its character of luxuriant productiveness from a portion of salt intimately blended with its constituents, which, from its tendency to effloresce in a warm sun, renders the compound peculiarly friable. This soil is deep, and has been accumulating for unknown ages, from the spoils of the Mexican mountains, (a species of natural annexation which the laws of nations have no power to regulate,) and the vast prairies which are washed by its upper courses.

The rich valley of the Red River is of a magnificent breadth, and for the most part, where it has not been cleared for cultivation, covered with a dense growth of forest trees. All the bayous of this river, which are very numerous, branching off in every direction, and intersecting every part of this luxuriant valley, partake of the fertilizing character of the main stream.*

There are few things among the works of nature, more remarkable than the *floating prairies*, which are found upon the lakes bordering upon the coast of the Gulf. They seem to have been formed by the natural aggregation of such veget-

---

* Many of the preceding statements are the result of an extensive personal observation ; for others, the work is indebted to McCulloch, a compilation of considerable value, but unfortunately, not always to be relied on as authority. In some points, he is glaringly incorrect.

able matter as lay suspended upon the surface of
the water, supplied with a light substratum of soil,
partly by its own decay and disintegration, and
partly by attracting around its roots and fibres the
alluvial treasures with which all these waters
abound. From this, various kinds of grass and
weeds have sprung up, the roots of which have
become firmly interwoven with the subjacent mass,
matting it completely together, and giving it all
the appearance of a substantial island. It is often
several inches in thickness, and so nearly resembles terra firma, that not only the sagacity of man,
but even animal instinct has been deceived by it.
These floating prairies are sometimes of great
extent, and are by no means confined to waters
comparatively shoal. They literally cover the
deeps in some cases, and a great deal of precau-
tion is necessary to avoid them, for, stable as they
look at a distance, they are as unsubstantial as
shadows, so that boats may oftentimes be forced
through them. They are less trustworthy than
quicksands, for the unlucky wight who should
adventure himself upon their deceitful appear-
ances, would find himself entangled in a net of
interminable extent, from which it would be impossible to extricate himself.

It may not be deemed presumption, perhaps, to
suggest, that the great Raft on the Red River
may be a formation upon the same principle,

though upon a more enlarged scale. The stream being sluggish, and the alluvial deposit exceedingly heavy and rich, the accumulation of a productive soil, and the consequent growth and entanglement of roots would be very rapid; and a foundation would ultimately be formed sufficiently stable and permanent, to be travelled with safety. Floating trees from the upper courses, arrested by this obstruction, would imbed themselves in the mass, until, by continual accretions, it should become what it now is, an impassable and almost irremovable barrier to navigation.

The Delta of the Mississippi is a region of extensive marshes. For many leagues, the lakes, inlets and sounds, which dissect and diversify that amphibious wilderness, are connected by an inextricable tissue of communications and passes, accessible only by small vessels and bay craft, and impossible to be navigated except by the most experienced pilots. It is a perfect labyrinth of waters, more difficult to unravel than those of Crete and Lemnos. The shore is indented by numberless small bays, or coves, few of which have sufficient depth of water, to afford a shelter for vessels. Berwick and Barritaria Bays are the only ones of any considerable magnitude.

The prairies which cover so large a portion of this State, are, for the most part, connected together, as if the waters from which they were originally deposited had been an immense chain of lakes, all fed from the same great source. And this was undoubtedly the fact. They were all supplied from the Mississippi, and their wonderful fertility is derived from the alluvial riches of those interminable regions, which are washed by the father of rivers and his countless tributaries. Those included under the general name of Attakapas, are the first which occur on the west of the Mississippi. It is an almost immeasurabie plain of grass, extending from the Atchafalaya on the north, to the Gulf of Mexico, on the south. Its contents are stated to be about five thousand square miles. Being open to the Gulf, it is generally fanned by its refreshing breezes. To the traveller in those regions, who may have been toiling on his weary way through tangle, and swamp, and forest, there is something indescribably agreeable in this smooth and boundless sea of unrivalled fertility, whose dim outline mingles with the blue of the far off Gulf—the whole vast plain covered with tall grass, waving and rippling in the breeze, sprinkled with neat white houses, the abodes of wealth, comfort and hospitality, and dotted with innumerable cattle and horses grazing in the fields, or reposing here and there under the shade of the wooded points. The sudden transition from the rank cane, the annoying nettles, the stifling air, and the pestilent mosquitoes, to this open expanse, and the cool salubrious breath of the ocean, is as delightful and reviving as an oasis in the desert.

In the midst of this immense prairie, is situated the parish of Attakapas. This word, in the language of the Aborigines, from whom it is derived, signified "man-eater," the region having been occupied by Cannibals. Strange indeed, that the inhabitants of a climate so bland, and a soil so fertile, should possess the taste, or feel the necessity for so revolting and unnatural a species of barbarism.

Opelousas prairie is still more extensive than Attakapas, being computed to contain nearly eight thousand square miles. It is divided by bayous, wooded grounds, points, and bends, and other natural boundaries, into a number of smaller prairies, which have separate names, and characteristics more or less distinctive. Taken in its whole extent, it is bounded by the Attakapas prairie on the east, pine woods and hill on the north, the Sabine on the west, and the Gulf of Mexico on the south. The soil though in many places extremely fertile, is generally less so than that of Attakapas. It has, however, a compensating advantage, being deemed the healthiest region in the State. It embraces several large cotton plantations, and a considerable region devoted to the cultivation of the sugar cane. The parish which bears its name is one of the most populous in Louisiana. It is the centre of the land of shepherds, the very Arcadia of those who deal in domestic animals. To that employment, the greater part of the inhabitants are devoted, and they number their flocks and herds by thousands. On one estate five thousand calves were branded in the spring of 1845.

The people of this district are distinguished for that quiet, easy, unostentatious hospitality, which assures the visitor of his welcome, and makes him so much at home, that he finds it difficult to realize that he is only a-guest.

Bellevue prairie lies partly in Opelousas, and partly in Attakapas. Calcasieu and Sabine prairies are only parts of the great plain, those names being given to designate some of the varied forms and openings it assumes in its ample sweep from the Plaquemine to the Sabine. They are, however, though but parts of a larger prairie, of immense extent. The Sabine, seen from any point near its centre, seems, like the mid-ocean, boundless to the view. The Calcasieu is seventy miles long, by twenty wide. Though, for the most part, so level as to have the aspect of a perfect plain, the surface is slightly undulated, with such a general, though imperceptible declination towards the streams and bayous by which it is intersected, as easily to carry off the water, and prevent those unhealthy stagnations which are so fatal in this climate. There is also a gentle slope towards the Gulf, along the shore of which the vast plain terminates in low marshes often entirely covered with the sea. These marshes are overspread with a luxuriant growth of tall reedy cane grass.

One of the most striking and peculiar features of these prairies is found in the occasional patches of timbered land, with which their monotonous surface is diversified and relieved. They are like islands in the bosom of the ocean, but are for the most part so regular and symmetrical in their forms, that one is with difficulty convinced that they are not artificial, planted by the hand of man, in circles, squares, or triangles, for mere ornament. It is impossible for one who has not seen them, to conceive of the effect produced by them, rising like towers of various forms, but each regular in itself, from the midst of an ocean of grass. Wherever a bayou or a stream crosses the prairie, its course is marked with a fringe of timber, the effect of which upon the eye of the observer is exceedingly picturesque, making a background to the view in many instances, like lines of trees in landscape painting.

All the rivers, bayous, and lakes of this State abound with alligators. On Red River, before it was navigated by steamboats, it was not uncommon to see hundreds in a group along the banks, or covering the immense masses of floating and stranded timber, bellowing like angry bulls, and huddled so closely together, that the smaller ones were obliged to get upon the backs of the larger. At one period, great numbers were killed for their skins, which were made into leather for boots and shoes, but not proving sufficiently close grained to keep out the water, the experiment was abandoned. Alligators average from eight to twelve feet in length. Some have been caught, measuring twenty feet.

The fear is often entertained, and sometimes expressed, that the levees of the Mississippi are not sufficient to resist the great body of water that is continually bearing and wearing upon them; and these fears have, in several cases, been realized, though never to any very great extent. In May 1816 the river broke through, about nine miles above New Orleans, destroyed several plantations, and inundated the back part of the city to the depth of three or four feet. The crevasse was finally closed, by sinking a vessel in the breach, for the suggestion and accomplishment of which, the public was chiefly indepted to Governor Claiborne.

In June, 1844, the river rose higher than it had done for many years, marking its whole course, for more than two thousand miles, with wide spread destruction to property and life. It crept over the levee in some places near New Orleans, but caused no actual breach in that vicinity. At Bonnet Carre it forced a crevasse, doing considerable damage and causing great alarm in the neighborhood; but the mischief was not so serious as might have been anticipated, and the embankment has been so increased and strengthened, as to leave but little apprehension for the future.

The interests of Education in Louisiana, though hitherto too much neglected, are now decidedly and preceptibly advancing. In the higher departments, are the College of Lousiana, at Jackson, in East Feliciana; and Jefferson College in St. James parish, on the coast—the former incorporated in 1825, the later in 1831. Both have at various times, received generous donations from the treasury of the state. Franklin College, in Opelousàs was also incorporated in 1831, under the same favorable auspices*

---

* The new constitution of Louisiana prescribes that the legislature shall establish free schools throughout the state, appoint a superintendent of education, and provide means for defraying the expense by taxation. The proceeds from the sale of all public lands granted by the United States, the estates of deceased persons escheating to the state, as well as certain other named emoluments, are to remain a perpetual fund, sacredly to be applied to the support of such schools. A provision is also to be made for establishing a college in the city of New Orleans, to be called *the University of Louisiana,* to consist of four faculties, viz. law, medicine, the natural sciences and letters—of which the Medical College of Louisiana, as now organized, is to constitute the faculty of medicine. The legislature is to be under no obligations to contribute to the support of this institution by appropriations.

There are also several Academies acting under the legal sanction of the State, although not endowed by it. The Ursuline Nuns' School and that of the Sisters of Charity—the latter in the parish of St. James, afford instruction in all the polite branches of female education. The Convent at Grand Coteau near Opelousas, has an average of about two hundred scholars; and efficient persons from France have the control and direction of their education.

The public schools, designed for the general and gratuitous dissemination of knowledge among all classes, have not only increased in number but have generaly outstripped those of the higher order, by seizing at once upon all the improvements which the experience of teachers in other parts of the country, and the world, has from time to time suggested. Mere innovations rather hinder than advance the progress of education. But the simplest suggestion of an enlightened experience and a sound judgment, such as are brought to bear upon this great interest throughout the whole of the nothern and eastern States, is entitled to the profound regard of the Southern philanthropist, whose aim and ambition it should be, to make the most of every facility and to be no whit behind the older, but not more wealthy sections, in any thing that can promote the moral and intellectual power of the masses of the people.

The climate of Louisiana is hot and moist. In the neighborhood of the marshes, and in the summer season, it partakes of the unhealthy character of nearly all tropical climates. Diseases of the lungs, however, and other complaints so prevalent at the north, are scarcely known; and to many, the quick consuming fever which finishes its work in a few days, may be considered but a fair offset to the slow but sure consumption, which flatters its victims with the semblance of life and hope, while dragging them through its long and dreary labyrinths, to the chambers of death.

This climate is favorable to almost all the productions of the tropics. The sugar, the cotton plant, the orange, the lemon, the grape, the mulbery, tobbaco, rice, maize, sweet potato, &c., &c., flourish in rich abundance, and some of them attain to a luxuriance of growth scarcely known in any other part of the world. Sugar and Cotton are the two great staples. The former is confined chiefly to that tract, which, by way of distinction, is called "the coast," lying along the shores of the Gulf, and the bayous of the Mississippi.

The average sugar crop of the whole state, is now about 180,000 hogsheads. That of cotton, for the last year is not ascertained, but the amount produced in the whole valley of the Mississippi, sent to New Orleans for export in 1843, was 1,088-000 bales. Owing to the large extension of the cot-

ton growing districts, and excessive competition in
its manufacture, the cultivation of cotton yields less
profit than it formerly did, and there seems to be
no substantial reason why it should not, in some degree, give place to sugar, at least until the latter
can be furnished in sufficient quantity to supply the
domestic consumption. Under the ordinary increase
of population, the utmost exertions of the cane planters will hardly arrive at such a result, in half a
century to come.

While on this subject, it will not, I trust, be
deemed irrelevant or officious, to place before the
reader the suggestions of an intelligent gentleman
of New Orleans, in regard to the present mode of
cultivating and manufacturing sugar. He observes
that in order to carry on the business to advantage,
and compete favorably with those already established, a large capital is required, since in addition
to the ground to be cultivated, and the hands to be
employed in the field, expensive mills and machinery must be set up, and kept in motion, with a large
number of laborers in attendance. Consequently
no man in moderate circumstances can undertake
this branch of business, as it is now conducted. To
obviate this difficulty, and extend the cultivation
and manufacture of this important staple, he pro-
poses a division of labor and profit, like that which
prevails in the grain growing and milling regions
of the north. The farmer sells his wheat, at a fair

market value, to the miller, or pays him a stipulated percentage for grinding and bolting. In the
same manner might the business here be divided
into two distinct branches. The planter might
sell his cane to the miller, or pay him the established price for converting it into sugar and molasses. This would enable men of comparatively
small means to undertake the cultivation of the
cane, who now confine themselves to cotton, and
thus relieve the larger cultivators of the latter
staple from the dangers of over production.

Casting our eyes back to no very distant period,
and noticing the small beginnings of our early
planters of cotton, the reader will pardon the in-
troduction of a trifling anecdote. During the year
1784, only sixty years since, and therefore within
the memory of many now living, an American
vessel, having *eighty bales* of cotton on board, was
seized at Liverpool, on the plea that *so large* an
amount of cotton could not have been produced
in the United States. The shipment in 1785
amounted to 14 bales, in 1786 to 6, in 1787 to
109, 1788 to 389, in 1789 to 842. An old Caro-
lina planter, having gathered his crop of five acres,
was so surprised and alarmed at the immense
amount they yielded, which was fifteen bales, that
he exclaimed " well, well—I have done with cot-
on—here is enough to make stockings for all the

people in America!" The cotton crop of the
United States for 1844 was 2,300,000 bales.

The fluctuations in the foreign cotton market,
within a few years past, have produced, among
scientific agriculturalists and experienced planters,
no little speculation upon the course which a due
regard to their own interests requires them to
pursue. It is not to be wondered at, that in a
country so vast, so luxuriantly fertile as ours, and
teeming with the most enterprising and industrious population on the face of the earth, the strict
relations of supply and demand should be occasionally disturbed in some of the many abundant
productions of the soil. It is always a difficult
problem to solve, especially where the field is
very large, and the producers many, and constantly increasing. In attempting to meet it, the first
question to be answered is, does the present supply
greatly overreach the present demand?

An intelligent writer in Hunt's Merchant's
Magazine for October, 1844, Henry Lee, Esq.,
has placed this subject, so far as he has there pursued it, in a very clear light. He commences by
stating that "the consumption of cotton in Europe,
other than the production of America and India,
is too insignificant to have any important bearing
upon prices." He goes on to show that the value
placed upon the article at present, is quite sufficient, and that the advantage it gives to the manu-

facturer of New England, whose operations are vastly increasing, renders him a successful competitor to those of Great Britain ; and nothing but an inflated currency, or imprudent speculations can produce an advance. And any advance so procured must inevitably be followed by a ruinous reaction. He shows that, through the agency of the British manufacturers, and the exporters of their goods to countries beyond the Cape of Good Hope, a considerable quantity of American grown cotton had been sent to those regions, in the form of manufactures and twist, over and above the amount of Indian grown cotton consumed in the factories of England. This simple fact, which is demonstrated as clearly as figures can speak, completely nullifies the importation of cotton from that quarter.

The proportion of raw cotton, other than the produce of the United States and India, used in the manufactures of Great Britain, is very small, and constantly diminishing in quantity. After producing statistical evidence, Mr. Lee arrives at the satisfactory result that the consumption of cotton from the United States and India, is as ninety-four to one hundred, leaving, for all other sources of supply, only six per cent. With such a ratio as this, and the competition constantly declining, it is manifest that we have nothing to fear from rival producers.

3

The delicate enquiry now arises, can the American planter sustain himself under existing prices? Or, can he, by the exercise of better economy, make his labors more productive? It seems to me, if it will not be presuming too far to offer the suggestion, that there should be an understanding between the larger and more intelligent planters, in relation to these points, and that they should, for their own individual and collective interests, consider, whether it would not be better partially to restrain the cultivation of this staple, rather than permit it to increase beyond the known and certain demands of commerce. The question increases in importance, as the cotton growing region enlarges, by the admission of "the lone star" into the constellation of Freedom. While it secures to the United States forever almost the entire monopoly of production, it puts it in her power, by a judicious combination among her great producers, to command a fair compensating price for cotton. Without some such combination, or, which is equivalent to the same thing, a prevailing disposition on the part of the planters, rather to wait for a demand than to anticipate, or endeavor to create it, there will always be a surplus stock in the market, which, however insignificant, will affect the price of the whole crop.

The luxuriant soil of Louisiana is capable of

of producing many articles even more lucrative than cotton, of which there is no immediate danger of creating an over supply. For some of them, there is a very large and increasing home consumption, as well as an active demand in other parts of the world that are open to our commerce. Of sugar, I have spoken already. Madder, silk, hemp, tobacco, may also be mentioned, as promising sure results to any who are disposed to try them. Under the impression that, in view of what I have already presented, the subject will be interesting to my readers, I shall venture to add a few words in relation to some of the above-mentioned articles.

Madder,* (*rubia tinctorum,*) the roots of a plant, which consist of several varieties. They are long and slender; varying from the thickness of a goose quill, to that of the little finger. They are semi-transparent, of a reddish color, have a strong smell, and a smooth bark. Madder is very extensively used in dying red; and, though the color which it imparts be less bright and beautiful than that of cochineal, it has the advantage of being cheaper and more durable. It is a native of the south of Europe, Asia Minor, and India; but has long since been introduced into,

---

* For many satisfactory particulars, see McCulloch's Commercial Dictionary, under article *Madder.*

and successfully cultivated in Holland, Alsace, Provence, &c. The attempt to cultivate it in England, like that of Indian corn, has proved a complete failure. The English, for a long time, depended upon Holland for their supplies; but now large quantities are imported from France and Turkey, under a duty of two shillings sterling on the manufactured, and sixpence on the roots. The duties, formerly, were much higher.

The plant is raised from seed, and requires three years to come to maturity. It is, however, often pulled in eighteen months, without injury to the quality, the quantity only being smaller. It requires a light vegetable mould, that retains the greatest quantity of water and adheres the least to the tools. When the soil is impregnated with an alkaline matter, the root acquires a red color, in other cases it is yellow. The latter is preferred in England, from the long habit of using Dutch madder, which is of this color; but in France, the red sells at a higher price, being used for Turkey red die.

The Zealand or Dutch madder is prepared for market in a manufactured state; and is known in trade by the terms, *mull, gamene, ombro,* and *crops.* In some other countries, the roots are packed up promiscuously, and the article is sold by the quintal. The price of madder, like every thing else, is affected by the quantity in market, and ranges in

France from its minimum 22, to 100 francs a quintal. It does not deteriorate by age. The quantity used in this country is very considerable—but nothing equal to that required in Great Britain. For the particular manner of cultivating madder, the reader is referred to an excellent essay upon that subject, from the pen of M. De Casparin, which was laid before the Academy of Sciences at Paris, and a prize awarded to its author.

The *mulberry* is grown with little difficulty in these latitudes, and therefore, silk may be produced in abundance, and rendered an article of domestic and commercial consequence. Plantations have already been commenced in several of the parishes, which will soon test the feasibility of the undertaking. A gentleman by the name of Vasseur, recently from France, has purchased land and made preparations to enter into that business, under many years of experience. In the parish of St. James, particularly, considerable attention is being paid to the culture of silk. It would be extremely gratifying to be able to lay the result of these experiments before the reader; but the necessary information is not at hand.

Hemp is raised in Missouri and Kentucky to some extent, as the quantities annually landed on the levee in New Orleans afford ample evidence. The demand for it will be good for many years, and the hint should not be neglected by the citizens of Louisiana, who possess the higher grounds, which are calculated for its production. When it is considered that this is a raw material of vast demand, which has heretofore been furnished from abroad, there can scarcely be any excuse for neglecting the culture, provided the profits be equal to those on sugar and cotton. The time may come, when even foreign nations will look to this republic for cordage and duck; at all events, we should not depend upon them for articles necessary for domestic purposes, and especially for those which may with propriety be classed " among the sinews of war."

Specimens of *tobacco,* the produce of seed imported from Cuba, have been exhibited in this market, which are very little, if any, inferior to the best from that island. These samples were raised by a gentleman who resides near Jackson, who took no extraordinary pains in the cultivation. The segars manufactured from them would pass, among good judges, for the best Havana. This planter is of opinion that he can very much improve the crops, by bestowing as much care upon them as is given to the same pursuit in Cuba, and there can be little reason to question his assertion.

The Natchitoches tobacco stands higher abroad, particularly for snuff, than any other. This article is so well known in France, and many other places, that those who are engaged in planting it, boast that it requires no protective duties, as it will be quite able to take care of itself.

The only drawback upon the cultivation of tobacco, in this state, is the worm, which begins its depredations in early summer. But much loss by this annoyance might be avoided, by forcing the plants in their early stage, in a hot-house, so that they might sooner be brought to maturity, and two clippings be made before the advent of the worm.

The thin soil on lake Pontchartrain is found to be well adapted to the *vine*. Already, considerable progress has been made in its cultivation in that neighbourhood, and grapes are abundantly furnished for the New Orleans market. There is no doubt that wine might be produced in abundance.

Indigo, one of the oldest products of this state, has been superseded by the sugar cane. Whether the planter has found more advantage in the latter than in the former cultivation, can only be inferred from his continuing to pursue it ; for the maxim, that trade will regulate itself, is nearly as applicable to agriculture as to commerce.

Grazing, although it has been carried to a great extent in Attakapas and Opelousas, has never proved so lucrative as might be supposed. Many of the cattle perish there during winter, for the want of proper nourishment. There is a grass, however, known by the name of *muskeet*, an ever-green, which flourishes abundantly in Texas, spreads rapidly, is exceedingly nutritious, and much sought for by animals, and might easily be introduced into these prairies. This improvement would make this section of country the best for grazing in the United States. More attention is being paid to breeding cattle, and the improvement of stock, than formerly. Sheep may be raised among the hills,. in and about Natchitoches, in almost any numbers. In Lafourche, also, al-though they are of small size, they are fat and of fine flavor. This is a business which is yet in its infancy here. The capabilities for its extension are immense, and there is no doubt that the enter-prise of the inhabitants will soon find means to make it profitable. The mutton of this state is already superior to any produced in the Union; good judges in these matters have even pronounced it to be equal to the best English.

The minerals of Louisiana, so far as known, are very limited. Lead has only been found in fragments; and none of these have proved to be rich. Valuable beds of gypseous marl exist in the vicinity of the Wachita, which admit of being worked to great advantage. Lignite coal has been discovered in tertiary formations, which never present any article of this kind beyond an ordina-ry quality, the better being always confined to the secondary strata. On the lands north of lake Pontchartrain, clay exists of an excellent quality and very pure, suitable for manufacturing not only the best bricks, but pottery of all kinds. It is to be hoped that this will remedy the great evil that New Orleans has hitherto experienced, by the use of a bad material for buildings. This has arisen from the employment of a substance too near the surface of the earth; whereas, by going a little deeper, a prime clay is obtained, that would bid defiance, when well burnt, to the humidity peculiar to this southern atmosphere.

3*

NEW ORLEANS.

Mouth of the Mississippi.

NEW ORLEANS, the capital of Louisiana, stands on the right side of the Mississippi, in ascending, ninety-two miles from its mouth. The river here makes a considerable bend to the northeast, and the city occupies the north-western side, although its situation is east of the general course of the stream. It is in latitude 29° 57′ north, longitude 90° 8′ west; by the river 301 miles below Natchez; 1220 miles below St. Louis; 1040 below Cairo, at the mouth of the Ohio; 2004 below

Pittsburg; and 1244 southwest from Washington city.

In 1718, Bienville, then governor of the province, explored the banks of the Mississippi, in order to choose a spot for the chief settlement, which had hitherto been at Biloxi. He selected the present site, and left fifty men to clear the ground, and erect the necessary buildings. Much opposition was made, both by the military and the directors of the Western Company, to removing the seat of government to this place. Another obstacle, for a while, threatened almost insurmountable difficulties to his design. In 1719, the Mississippi rose to an extraordinary height; and, as the company did not possess sufficient force to protect the spot from inundation, by dykes and levees, it was for a time abandoned. In the November of 1722, however, in pursuance of orders, Delorme removed the principal establishment to New Orleans. In the following year, agreeably to Charlevoix, it consisted only of one hundred cabins, placed with little order, a large wooden warehouse, two or three dwelling-houses, and a miserable store-house, which had been used as a chapel, a mere shed being then the only accommodation afforded for a house of prayer. The population did not exceed two hundred Thus commenced what is now called the "Crescent city;" which, in a commercial point of view, and

in proportion to the number of its inhabitants, has
not an equal upon the face of the globe.

During the same year, a party of German emigrants, who had been disappointed by the financier,
Law, of settling on lands granted to him in Arkansas, descended the river to New Orleans, in
the hope of obtaining passage to France; but the
government being either unwilling or unable to
grant it, small allotments of land were apportioned
them, on what is now called the German Coast.
These people supplied the city with garden stuffs;
and most of their descendants, with large acces-
sions from the old country, still cultivate the same
land, upon a much improved scale.

In September of this year, the capital was
visited by a terrible hurricane, which levelled to the
ground the church, if such it might be called, the
hospital, and thirty houses; and three vessels that
lay in the river were driven ashore. So destructive
was it to the crops and gardens, that a scarcity of
provisions was the consequence; and such was
the distress, that several of the inhabitants seriously
thought of abandoning the colony.

In the summer of 1727, the Jesuits and Ursuline
nuns arrived. The fathers were placed on a tract
of land now forming the lowest part of the fauxbourg St. Mary. The nuns were temporarily
lodged in a house in the corner of Chartres and
Bienville streets—but, soon after, the company laid

the foundation of the edifice in Conde and Ursuline streets, to which they were removed in 1730 ; this place was occupied by them until the great value of the land induced them to divide the larger portion of it into lots. Their new convent was erected about two miles below the city, and there they removed in 1824. At this period, the council house and jail were built, on the upper side of the Cathedral.

In 1763, Clement XIII expelled the Jesuits from the dominions of the kings of France, Spain and Naples. They were, consequently, obliged to leave Louisiana. Their property in New Orleans was seized, and sold for about one hundred and eighty thousand dollars. It is now estimated to be worth upwards of fifteen millions. At the time of the expulsion of this order, they owned the grounds which are now occupied by the second municipality. The valuable buildings in which they dwelt, were situated in Gravier and Magazine streets. Some of them were pulled down to make room for the late banking house of the Canal bank, on the corner of those streets. It is computed, that more than one half of the real estate in this city, is derived from the confiscation of the property of the Jesuits, under legal proceedings had by order of the French government. The archives of the first municipality contain many interesting and curious documents in relation to these proceedings, that are well worth examination.

The first visitation of the yellow fever was in 1769. Since that time it has continued to be almost an annual scourge. It was introduced into this continent, in the above named year, *by a British vessel,* from the coast of Africa, *with a cargo of slaves.* In addition to this affliction, (the yellow fever above alluded to,) the colony was, during the year 1769, transferred to Spain, and the capital was taken possession of by O ' Reilly, with a show of military power, and an individual diposition to oppress, that brought equal disgrace upon himself, and upon the government that commissioned him. The commerce of this city suffered very much from the restrictive colonial system of Spain. This, however, was removed in 1778, (a year memorable for a fire that burnt nine hundred houses at one time) and, in 1782, the mercantile interest of the place was benefited by still further extended privileges of trade.

The census of 1785 gives to the city a population of 4,780, exclusive of the settlements in the immediate vicinity.

In consequence of the commercial advantages above alluded to, a number of merchants from France established themselves here, and British trading vessels navigated the Mississippi. They were a species of marine pedlars, stopping to trade at any house, by making fast to a tree, and receiving in payment for merchandize, whatever the

planter had to spare, or giving him long credits.
The Americans, at that time, commenced the
establishment of that trade from the west to New
Orleans, which has been steadily increasing ever
since. The idea of this traffic was first conceived
by General Wilkinson. A lucrative business was
also conducted by the Philadelphians, which the
colonial authorities winked at for a while ; but the
Spanish minister, finding that he did not participate
in the profits of it, as the Americans refused to com-
ply with his hints to consign to his friends, put a
stop to it. He procured a list of the names of
the vessels, severely reprimanded the intendant,
Navarro, and so worked upon his fears that he
began to prosecute all infringements of the revenue laws, seizing the vessels, confiscating the goods
and imprisoning the owners, captains and crews.
The venal minister, perceiving that he had rendered
himself extremely unpopular by his intermeddling
with the commerce between Philadelphia and New-
Orleans, finally released all the individuals he
had imprisoned, restoring the confiscated property, and discontinuing any further interference.
The trade immediately received a new impulse
and was greatly increased. General Wilkinson at
the same time obtained permission to send one or
more launches loaded with tobacco, from Kentucky.

Soon after, many Americans availed themselves

of a privilege which was granted, of settling in the country.

The first company of French comedians arrived here in 1791. They came from Cape Francois, whence they made their escape from the revolted slaves. Others from the same quarter opened academies—the education of youth having hitherto been confined to the priests and nuns.

The baron Carondelet, in 1792, divided the city into four wards. He recommended lighting it, and employing watchmen. The revenue did not amount to seven thousand dollars, and to meet the charges for the purchase of lamps and oil, and to to pay watchmen, a tax of one dollar and an eighth was levied upon chimneys.

He also commenced new fortifications around the capital. A fort was erected where the mint now stands, and another at the foot of Canal street. A strong redoubt was built in Rampart street, and at each of the angles of the now city proper. The Baron also paid some attention to training the militia. In the city, there were four companies of volunteers, one of artillery, and two of riflemen, consisting of one hundred men each, making an aggregate force of 700 men.

A great extension was given to business in February of this year. The inhabitants were now permitted to trade freely in Europe and America, wherever Spain had formed treaties for the regulation of commerce. The merchandise thus imported, was subject to a duty of fifteen per cent; and exports to six per cent. With the Peninsula it was free.

In 1795 permission was granted by the king to citizens of the United States, during a period of ten years, to deposit merchandise at New Orleans. The succeeding year, the city was visited by another conflagration, which destroyed many houses. This reduced the tax upon chimneys so much, that recourse was had to assessing wheat, bread and meat, to defray the expense of the city light and watch.

At the time of the transfer to the United States, the public property consisted of two large brick stores, running from the levee on each side of Main street, (which were burnt in 1822,)—a government house, at the corner of Levee and Toulouse streets, (which also suffered a similar fate in 1826,)—a military hospital, and a powder magazine, on the opposite side of the river, which was abandoned a few years since—an old frame custom house—extensive barracks below those now remaining—five miserable redoubts, a town house, market house, assembly room and prison, a cathedral and presbytery, and a charity hospital. At this memorable era, the grounds which now constitute that thriving portion of the city, known as the second municipality, were mostly used as a plantation. It was the property of a wealthy citizen named Gravier, after whom one of the principal streets that runs through the property has been called. How has the scene changed? At this moment it contains a population of nearly fifty thousand, and has become the centre of the business, and enterprize, and beauty of the city.

In 1804 New Orleans was made a port of entry and delivery, and Bayou St. John a port of delivery. The first act of incorporation was granted to the city, by the legislative council of the territory, in 1805, under the style of " the Mayor, Aldermen and inhabitants of the city of New Orleans." The officers were a mayor, recorder, fourteen aldermen, and a treasurer. This year, a branch of the United States bank was established in this capital.

The population of the city and suburbs, in 1810, amounted to 24,552 ; having been trebled in seven years, under the administration of its new government. The prosperity of its trade increased in an equal ratio.

At that time, the city extended no further down than Esplanade street, with the exception of here and there a villa scattered along the levee ; nor above, further than Canal street, unless occasionally a house occupying a square of ground. A few dwellings had been erected on Canal and Magazine streets, but it was considered to be getting quite into the country, to go beyond the *Polar Star Lodge*, which was at the corner of Camp and Gravier streets. [The progress of this municipality has been greatly increased by the act for the division of the city, passed by the Legislature in 1836, by which the second municipality acquired the exclusive control of its own affairs.]

There was not then a paved street in the city. The late Benjamin Morgan, who, some time after, made the first attempt, was looked upon as a visionary. The circumstance which gave an impulse to improvements in the second municipality, was the erection of the American theatre, on Camp street, by James H. Caldwell, Esq., the only access to which, for long a time, was over flat-boat gunwales. This was in 1823–4. He was ridiculed for his folly, and derided as a madman—but time proved his foresight. He was soon followed by a crowd that gave life and energy to that section; and, in a few years, through the enterprise of others of a similar spirit, the suburb of St. Mary has reached to its present advanced state of elegance and prosperity.

The block where the Merchants' Exchange has since been built, was then occupied by a row of frail wooden shanties; and the corner of Royal and Custom house streets, where the bank now stands, was tenanted by Scot, who now furnishes food for his hundreds a day directly opposite, and

who laid the foundation of his fortune, in the tene-
ment that was removed to make room for the present beautiful edifice.

Some of the old Frenchmen in the city proper,
who have rarely trusted themselves three squares
beyond their favorite cabaret, are very incredulous
of the reported progress and improvement in the
fauxbourg St. Mary. A few years since, a gentleman of the second municipality asked the old
cabaret keeper, who has made himself illustrious
and wealthy by vending, to the habitués of the
lower market, a drink of his own compounding,
called *pig and whistle*—why he did not come up
into the fauxbourg St. Mary, and see the buildings?
—at the same time describing the St. Charles Exchange, the Theatre, the Verandah, Banks' Arcade,
the magnificent stores, &c. The old Frenchman,
listened in doubting wonder for some time; at
last, however, his faith and his gravity both gave
way, and he burst into a laugh, exclaiming, " ah
Monsieur B. dat is too much! You von varry
funny fellow—I no believe vat you say—its only
von grand—vot you call it—vere de mud, de alligator, and de bull frog live ?—von grand—grand
—mud swamp, vere you say is von grand city, I
no believe it !"

The city proper is bounded by Canal, Rampart,
and Esplanade streets, and on the river by the
levee, on which it extended about thirteen hundred

yards, and back about seven hundred—in the form of a parallelogram.

This portion is traversed by twenty-two streets, forming eighty-four principal and fourteen minor squares. The whole extent of the city, including the incorporated fauxbourgs and Lafayette, is not less than five miles on a line with the river, and running an average of half a mile in width.

The houses are chiefly constructed with bricks, except a few ancient and dilapidated dwellings in the heart of the city, and some new ones in the outskirts. Wooden buildings are not permitted to be built, under present regulations, within what are denominated the fire limits. The modern structures, particularly in the second municipality, are generally three and four stories high, and are embellished with handsome and substantial granite or marble fronts. The public buildings are numerous ; and many of them will vie with any of the kind in our sister cities. A particular description of these will be found in the ensuing pages.

The view of New Orleans from the river, in ascending or descending, is beautiful and imposing—seen from the dome of the St. Charles Exchange, it presents a panorama at once magnificent and surprising. In taking a lounge through the lower part of the city, the stranger finds a difficulty in believing himself to be in an American city. The older buildings are of ancient and foreign construction, and the manners, customs and language are various—the population being composed, in nearly equal proportions, of American, French, Creoles, and Spaniards, together with a large portion of Germans, and a good sprinkling from almost every other nation upon the globe.

The Water Works constantly supply the people with water forced from the Mississippi, by the agency of steam, into a reservoir, whence by pipes it is sent all over the city. This water is wholesome and palatable.

Gas was introduced into New Orleans, through the enterprize of James H. Caldwell, Esq., in 1834 ; he having lighted his theatre with it several years previous. The dense part of the city is now lighted by it ; and the hotels, stores, shops, and many dwelling-houses within reach, have availed themselves of the advantages it offers.

In the summer of 1844, a fire destroyed about seven blocks of buildings between Common and Canal streets, near the charity Hospital. The ground has since been occupied with much better buildings, and presents a very improved appearance.

The population of New Orleans, after it was ceded to the United States, increased very rapidly. At the time of the transfer, there were not eight thousand inhabitants.

		Blacks.	Whites.	Total.
In	1810	8001	16,551	24,552
	1815	—	—	32,947
	1820	19,737	21,614	41,350
	1825	—	—	45,336
	1830	21,280	28,530	49,826
	1840	—	—	102,191

and, at the present period there are, probably one hundred and thirty thousand. During 1844 there were more buildings erected than any previous year—notwithstanding which, tenements are in great demand, and rents continue high. It will not be a matter of surprize, if the number of inhabitants at the next census, 1850, should be over one hundred and sixty thousand.

The first ordinance for the establishment of a board of health in this city, (so far as known,)was passed by the general council in June, of 1841.* The board consisted of nine members—three aldermen, three physicians, and three private citizens. It was invested with ample powers to adopt and enforce such sanitary regulations as were thought conducive to the health of the city. This board performed all its functions well during the first year of its existence. The second year there was a falling off; but a dissolution did not take place till 1843. In 1844, the board of health

---

* See New Orleans Medical Journal, vol. 1, part 2, July, 1844.

having ceased to officiate, the general council invited the medico-chirurgical society to take charge of this duty. This proposition was accepted, and a committee of nine members appointed, with full power to act as a board of health. If this body do their duty, as there is no reason to doubt they will, much benefit may be expected to result. Their advice to citizens, and strangers who were unacclimated, on the approach of the warm weather of 1844, was certainly marked with a great degree of good sense and seasonable caution. They will now be looked up to as the great conservators of the health of the city; and, it is to be hoped that public expectation will not be disappointed.

The following abstract of a Meteorological Journal for 1844 was obligingly furnished by D. T. Lillie, Esq., of New Orleans, a gentleman whose scientific acquirements are a sure guaranty for its accuracy. The thermometer (a self registering one) used for these observations, is not attached to the barometer, and is placed in a fair exposure. Hours of observation, 8 A. M., 2 P. M., and 8 P. M. The barometer is located at an elevation of 28 feet above the level of the ocean; and is suspended clear of the wall of the building. The rain guage is graduated to the thousandth part of an inch, and the receiver of it is elevated 40 feet from the ground.

METEOROLOGICAL TABLE.

1844. Months.	Thermometer.			Barometer.			Rainy Days.	Prevailing Winds.	Force of Winds, ratio 1 to 10.	Quan. of Rain.	
	Max. 0 tenths.	Min. 0 tenths.	Range, 0 tenths.	Max. 0 hund.	Min. 0 hund.	Range, 0 hund.				Inches.	Thousands.
January,	79.5	36.5	43.0	30.38	29.73	0.65	11	S. E.	2.4	4	966
February,	81.0	40.0	41.0	30.40	29.91	0.49	5	S. E.	2.4	0	879
March,	83.0	38.0	45.0	30.40	29.83	0.57	9	N. W.	3.0	3	031
April,	85.0	40.0	45.0	30.46	29.98	0.48	3	S. E.	2.5	1	797
May,	88.5	66.0	22.5	30.31	29.83	0.48	9	S. W.	2.7	4	847
June,	91.0	69.0	22.0	30.18	30 03	0.15	12	S.	2.3	5	789
July,	92.5	73.0	19.5	30.22	30.01	0.21	16	S. W.	2.2	9	801
August,	92.5	69.0	23.5	30 26	29.93	0.33	14	S. W.	2.4	5	199
September,	91.5	61.0	30.5	30.23	29 95	0 28	8	E.	2.5	1	080
October,	85.5	46.0	39.5	30.31	29.89	0.42	4	N. E.	2.5	2	180
November,	74.0	40.0	34.0	30.34	29.94	0.40	9	N.	2.2	7	754
December,	74.5	32.5	42.0	30.44	29.83	0.61	4	N.	2.4	1	077
Ann'l Mean,	84.9	50.9	33.9	30.33	29.90	0.42	104		2.5	48	400

Annual range of the thermometer 60 degrees 0 minutes—of the barometer 00. degrees 73 hundreths.

Society, as at present constituted in New Orleans, has very little resemblance to that of any other city in the Union. It is made up of a heterogeneous mixture of almost all nations. First, and foremost, is the Creole population. All who are born here, come under this designation, without reference to the birth place of their parents. They form the foundation, on which the superstructure of what is termed "society," is erected. They are remarkably exclusive in their intercourse with others, and, with strangers, enter into business arrangements with extreme caution. They were

4

once, and very properly, considered as the patricians of the land. But they are not more distinguished for their exclusiveness, and pride of family, than for their habits of punctuality, temperance, and good faith.

Till about the commencement of the present century, the period of the transfer of Louisiana to the United States, the Creoles were almost entirely of French and Spanish parentage. Now, the industrious Germans, the shrewd and persevering Irishmen, are beginning to be quite numerous, and many of them have advanced to a condition of wealth and respectability.

Next come the emigrants from the sister States, from the mighty west, from the older sections of the south, and (last not least) from the colder regions of the north, the enterprising, calculating, hardy Yankee. To the latter class this emporium is indebted, for many of those vast improvements which, as if by magic, have risen to the astonishment and confusion of those of the ancient regime, who live in a kind of seclusion within the limits of the *city proper*—to whom beautiful and extensive blocks of buildings have appeared in the morning, as though they had sprung up by enchantment during the night.

Then come the nondescript watermen. Our river steam navigation, averaging, during half the year, some three hundred arrivals per month, furnishes a class of ten thousand men, who have few if any parallels in the world. The numberless flat-boats that throng the levees for an immense distance, are peopled and managed by an amphibious race of human beings, whose mode of living is much like that of the alligator, with whom they ironically claim relationship, but who carry under their rough exterior and uncouth manners, a heart as generous and noble, as beats in any human breast. They are the children of the Mississippi, as the Arabs are of the great desert, and, like them, accustomed to encounter danger in every shape. Combining all the most striking peculiarities of the common sailor, the whaleman, the backwoodsman, and the Yankee, without imitating, or particularly resembling any one of them, they are a class en tirely by themselves, unique, eccentric, original, a distinct and unmistakeable feature in the floating mass that swarms on the levees, and threads the streets, of the cresent city.

Among them may be found the representatives of nearly all the states. Some are descendants of the Pilgrims, and have carried with them the industrious habits, and the strict moral princi-ples, of their Puritan forefathers, into the wilds of the West. They are all active, enterpri-sing, fearless, shrewd, independent, and self-suffi-cient, and often aspiring and ambitious, as our halls of legislation, and our highest business circles

can testify. They are just the stuff to lay the
broad foundations of freedom in a new country
—able to clear the forest, and till the soil, in time
of peace, to defend it in war, and to govern it at
all times.

Of the one hundred and thirty thousand souls,
who now occupy this capital, about twenty thousand
may be estimated as migratory. These are principally males, engaged in the various departments
of business. Some of them have families at the
North, where they pass the summer. Many are
bachelors, who have no home for one half the year,
and, if the poets are to be believed, less than half
a home for the remainder. As these two classes
of migratory citizens, who live at the hotels and
boarding houses, embrace nearly, if not quite, one
half the business men of the city, it may serve to
some extent, to account for the seemingly severe restrictions by which the avenues to good native society are protected. Unexceptionable character,
certified beyond mistake, is the only passport to the
domestic circle of the Creole. With such creden-
tials their hospitality knows no limits. The resident Americans are less suspicious in admitting you
to their hospitality, though not more liberal than
their Creole neighbors, when once their confidence
is secured.

The restrictions thus thrown around society, and
the great difficulty which the new comer experien-

ces in securing a share in those social enjoyments
to which he has been accustomed in other places,
have had an unfavorable effect upon the morals
of the place. Having no other resource for pas-
time, when the hours of business are over, he flies
to such public entertainments as the city affords.
And if these are not always what they should
be, it behooves us to provide better. Public libra-
ries, reading rooms, galleries for the exhibition of
the fine arts, lyceums for lectures, and other
kindred rational amusements, would do much to
establish a new and better order, and to break
down those artificial barriers, which separate so
many refined and pure minded men from the
pleasures and advantages of general society, con-
demning them to live alone and secluded, in
the midst of all that is lovely and attractive in the
social relations of life.

The character of New-Orleans, in respect to
health, has been much and unjustly abused. At
the north, in ratio to their population, the consumption annually destroys more than the yellow fever
of the south. The city of New York averages
about thirty a week. Patients with pulmonary
complaints, resort to these latitudes for relief,
where such diseases are otherwise rarely known.
In truth, this capital shows a more favourable bill
of mortality, than any seaport town in the United
States, except Charleston and Baltimore.

There is little to be said in favor of the morals of New Orleans, during the first few years after its cession. Report made them much worse than they were. As the community was composed of some of the worst classes of society, gathered from every region under the sun, nothing very good was to be expected. But circumstances have changed. A system of wholesome police regulations has been introduced and enforced, which has either brought the desperate and the lawless under subjection, or expelled them from the community. By reference to the statistics of crime, in other commercial cities in proportion to the number of inhabitants, the stranger will be convinced that this City has reason to be proud of her standing. Riots here are unknown, robberies seldom occur. Personal security in the public streets, at all hours, is never endangered—and females may venture out after dark, without a protector, and be free from insult and molestation. Foreign influence has entailed upon society here a *code of honor*, which, in some measure, has had a tendency to injure it, but the false notion is fast falling into disrepute.

The new state constitution, if adopted, will put an effectual stop to this barbarous practice. Article 130, reads,

"Any Citizen of this State who shall, after the adoption of this constitution, fight a duel with deadly weapons, or send a challenge to fight a duel, either within the state, or out of it, or who shall act as second, or knowingly aid and assist in any manner those thus offending, shall be deprived of holding any office of trust or profit, and of enjoying the right of suffrage under this Constitution."

The learned professions here, generally, stand preeminently high. The science of medicine may boast of a talent, and a skill, that would confer honor upon any city in the Union—and the few empirics who disgrace the practice, are so well known, that the evil is circumscribed within very narrow limits. The clergy are proverbial for their learning and eloquence—and the same remarks will apply with equal force to the members of the bar.

This city, at the present time, possesses no public library. Considering the population, and their ability, this must be regarded as a blot upon the intelligence of its citizens. This is completely a commercial community, however, and money is the universal ambition. Thence springs that acknowledged deficiency in literature and the fine arts, observable to the stranger. But shall it still remain? Is there no Girard—no Astor—among our millionaires, who will leave behind them a monument which shall make their names dearer and more honored in all coming time, than those of heroes and conquerors?

After several attempts to establish a library, an association of young men, some years ago, at last succeeded in organizing one ; but, for want of proper aid and support from the rich, it lingered on for some time, and was finally sold out by the sheriff!   It then consisted of four or five thousand volumes of well selected books.   It was purchased by a private gentleman, B. F. French, Esq. for a mere nominal sum.   Thus has a work intended for the honor of the city, become, in an evil hour, the monument of its shame !   It is soothing however, to learn that, at length, a love of letters and the fine arts is springing up in our midst. Under the head of Lyceums, National Gallery of Paintings, and Public Schools, in this volume, facts illustrative of this assertion may be seen.

The Masonic fraternity in New Orleans appear to enjoy all their ancient privileges.   There are some ten lodges, besides a grand lodge, and an encampment.   Here is a large number of the order of Odd Fellows, as one of Equal Fellows—a Typographical Association, and Mechanics, Hibernian, St. Andrews, German, and Swiss societies.   These are all, more or less, of a benevolent nature ; and within their own circles, have all been extremely serviceable.

The navigation of the Mississippi, even by steam boats, in 1818, was extremely tedious.   The Etna is recorded as arriving at Shipping port, a few miles below Louisville, in *thirty two* days.   The Governor Shelby in *twenty two* days, was considered as a remarkably short passage. An hermaphrodite brig was *seventy one* days from New Orleans—and a keel boat *one hundred and one;* the latter to Louisville. Now, the time occupied is *five to six* days.

During the business season, which continues from the first of November to July, the levee, for an extent of five miles, is crowded with vessels of all sizes, but more especially ships, from every part of the world—with hundreds of immense floating castles and palaces, called steam boats; and barges and flat boats innumerable. No place can present a more busy, bustling scene. The loading and unloading of vessels and steam boats—the transportation, by some three thousand drays, of cotton, sugar, tobacco, and the various and extensive produce of the great west, strikes the stranger with wonder and admiration. The levee and piers that range along the whole length of the city, extending back on an average of some two hundred feet, are continually covered with moving merchandize. This was once a pleasant promenade, where the citizen enjoyed his delightful morning and evening walk; but now there is scarcely room, amid hogsheads, bales and boxes, for the business man to crowd along, without a sharp look out for his personal safety.

The position of New Orleans, as a vast commercial emporium, is unrivalled—as will be seen

4*

by a single glance at the map of the United States.
As the depot of the west, and the half-way-house
of foreign trade, it is almost impossible to anticipate
its future magnitude.

Take a view, for instance, of the immense regions
known under the name of the Mississippi valley.
Its boundaries on the west are the Rocky Mountains, and Mexico ; on the south, the Gulf of
Mexico ; on the east the Alleghany mountains ;
and, on the north, the lakes and the British possessions. It contains nearly as many square miles,
and more tillable ground, than all continental Europe, and, if peopled as densely as England, would
sustain a population of five hundred millions—more
than half of the present inhabitants of the earth.
Its surface is generally cultivable, and its soil
rich, with a climate varying to suit all products,
for home consumption or a foreign market. The
Mississippi is navigable twenty one hundred miles
—passing a small portage, three thousand may be
achieved. It embraces the productions of many
climates, and a mining country abounding in coal,
lead, iron and copper ore, all found in veins of
wonderful richness. The Missouri stretches thirty nine hundred miles to the Great Falls, among
the Flat Foot Indians, and five thousand from
New Orleans. The Yellow Stone, navigable for
eleven hundred miles, the Platte for sixteen hundred, and the Kanzas for twelve hundred, are only

tributaries to the latter river. The Ohio is two thousand miles to Pittsburgh, receiving into her bosom from numerous streams, the products of New York, Pennsylvania, Ohio, Kentucky, Western Virginia, Tennesee, Indiana and Illinois. The Arkansas, Big Black, Yazoo, Red River, and many others, all pouring their wealth into the main artery, the Mississippi, upon whose mighty current it floats down to the grand reservoir, New Orleans.

The Mississippi valley contained over eight millions of inhabitants in 1840, having gained eighty per cent., during the last ten years. The present number cannot be less than ten millions.

The last year, the Mississippi was navigated by four hundred and fifty steam boats, many of which are capable of carrying 2,500 bales of cotton, making an aggregate tonnage of ninety thousand. They cost above seven millions of dollars ; and to navigate them, required nearly fifteen thousand persons—the estimated expense of their navigation is over thirteen millions of dollars. The increase since, may be calculated at fifty additional boats— which would make an advance in all these items in a ratio of ten per cent.

Such statements as these, large as they seem, convey to the reader but a partial idea of the great valley, and of the wide extent of country upon which this city leans, and which guaranties her present and future prosperity. To form a full

estimate, he must, besides all this, see her mountains of iron, and her inexhaustible veins of lead
and copper ore, and almost boundless regions of
coal.   The first article mentioned (and the phrase
in which it is expressed is no figure of speech) has
been pronounced, by the most scientific assayer of
France, to be superior to the best Swedish iron.
These, and a thousand unenumerated products,
beside the well known staples, constitute its wealth;
all of which by a necessity of nature, must flow
through our Cresent City, to find an outlet into the
great world of commerce.   With such resources
nothing short of some dreadful convulsion of nature, or the more dreadful calamity of war, can prevent New Orleans from becoming, if not the first,
next in commercial importance to the first city
in the United States—perhaps, in the world.   The
flourishing towns upon the Mississippi and her tributaries, are merely the depositories for this great
mart.   In twenty years she must, according to her
present increase, contain a population of three hundred thousand, with a trade proportionably extended.

With such views, it may be deemed folly to
attempt to look forward to the end of the nineteenth century, when this metropolis will in all
probability extend back to lake Pontchartrain, and
to Carrolton on the course of the river.   The
swamps, that now only echo to the hoarse bellowing of the alligator, will then be densely built upon,

and rendered cheerful by the gay voices of its inhabitants, numbering at least *a million of human beings*. If, like Rip Van Winkle, we may be permitted to come back after the lapse of half a century, with what surprize and astonishment shall we witness the change which the enterprize of man will have wrought. But let us not waste a moment in dreaming about it. Let us be up and doing, to fulfil our part of the mighty achievement. It would not be strange, however, if the present map, which is given to show the rapid growth of the city, by comparison with one drawn in 1728, should then be republished with a similar design, to exhibit the insignificance of New Orleans in 1845! We ask the kindness of the critics of that period, should they deign to turn over these pages, begging them to consider that our humble work was produced as far back as the benighted age of steam!

PUBLIC BUILDINGS.

—

HAVING noticed, in the preceding sketch, the most prominent features in the history of this interesting section of country, it becomes a duty now to present to the intelligent reader, and more especially to the inquiring traveler, a description of such of the public institutions, buildings, and places of resort, for business and amusement, as may be deemed worthy of his attention. In attaining this object, it was necessary to have recourse to the most carefully digested statements of facts now existing, as well as to collect others from personal inspection.

THE UNITED STATES BARRACKS.

The buildings formerly used for the accommodation of the troops garrisoned in New Orleans, were erected by the French about a century since. These were directed to be sold in 1828, and ten years after were demolished. The act was soon discovered to be an error, and in 1833, the goverment determined to replace them. A plan was accordingly forwarded to the seat of government and approved. On account of the difficulty of obtaining a suitable site within the incorporated limits, a location was selected, by assistant quarter master Drane, about three miles below the city. The works were begun the 24th of February, 1834, and completed on the 1st of December, 1835, at a cost, including the enclosure of the public grounds, of $182,000. The late Assistant quarter master J. Clark, superintended the operation, aided by Lieutenant J. Wilkinson, who had furnished the plans.

The Barracks occupy a parallelogram of about three hundred feet on the river, by nine hundred in depth. The ground in the rear belongs to the general government, to the depth of forty arpents, and can be used for the benefit of the troops. The garrison was intended to consist of four companies of infantry, but ample accomodation exists for a much larger number. The quarters of the commandant occupy the middle of the front ; those of the staff and company officers being on either flank. The companies are quartered in a hollow square, which is thrown back far enough to give space for a handsome parade ground. In the rear of these quarters are the hospital, storehouse, and corps des garde, and still in rear, and beyond the walls, is the post magazine, as well as other buildings necessary for the comfort and convenience of the troops. In front of the whole is a commodious wharf for the landing of supplies.

THE UNITED STATES BRANCH MINT

Is situated on what was once called Jackson Square, being nearly the former site of fort St. Charles. It is an edifice of the Ionic order, of brick plastered to imitate granite, having a centre building projecting, with two wings; is strongly built, with very thick walls, and well finished. Our limits will not permit us to go into a detailed description of its interior arrangements; which, however, may be generally spoken of as such as not to discredit the distinguished engineer who planned them. The total length of the edifice is 282 feet, and the depth about 108—the wings being 29 by 81, and the whole three stories in height. It was begun in September, 1835; and the building was perfectly completed at a cost of $182,000. The machinery is elegant and highly finished, and, when in operation, proves an interesting sight to visitors; which, from the gentlemanly urbanity of the officers of the establishment, may be easily enjoyed. The square is surrounded by a neat iron railing on a granite basement. The coinage of 1844—gold, $3,010,000—silver, $1,198,500—making in all $4,208,500.

THE CUSTOM HOUSE.

This establishment is conducted in an old building, quite too small, even if the United States Courts did not occupy a considerable portion of it. The square, in the centre of which it stands, is about 300 feet each on Old Levee, Custom-House, Front-Levee and Canal streets; and, from its peculiarly happy location, is well calculated for public improvement. Considering the great commercial importance of New-Orleans, as being scarcely second to any city in the Union, it is a matter of congratulation that the government are now disposed to place her upon a more respectable footing, in regard to offices of this nature; which have been furnished in a princely style to some of the sea-ports that had less need of them. The immense revenue that flows into the treasury department here, demands a suitable edifice for the transaction of the business it creates. The site is the most eligible that can be imagined. The Post-Office, United States Courts, and warehouses for

the storage of bonded merchandize, can all have
ample accommodation within its limits; and a more
desirable location for them cannot be found.   An
appropriation of $500 was made at the last
session of Congress, to secure a suitable plan for
the buildings to cover this spot.   The plan has
been prepared by Mr. Gallier, and is highly approved by those who have examined it.   It is to
be hoped there will be no unnecessary delay in
completing a work, in which the public convenience and economy, as well the accommodation of
the mercantile community, is so deeply interested.   If Mr. Gallier's plan is adopted, all the
above departments will be clustered together in
one central spot, with ample room for each, and
in a structure that will be at the same time a durable ornament to the city, and an honor to the
nation.

THE POST OFFICE,

Is located in the Merchants' Exchange.   It
has two business fronts, besides a passage way
through the building, where letters and packages
are received for mailing.   The private boxes have
their delivery here, where also the publishers of
newspapers receive their exchanges and communications.   The general delivery for English letters is in Exchange Place, those for letters in the
foreign languages, and for the ladies, are on Royal

street. The edifice seems to answer the purpose well ; and, considering the extent of the establishment, the duties of the office have been managed much to the satisfaction of the public. But we look for something more worthy of the place, when the new Custom House shall rear its noble front to the *father of rivers.*

THE STATE HOUSE,

Formerly the Charity Hospital, and purchased by the state in 1834, is a plain structure, composed of a centre and two detached wings ; and is finely situated on the square enclosed by Canal, Baronne, Common and Philippa streets. The main entrance to the square, which is laid off as a pleasure ground, and well kept, is from Canal street. The principal building is occupied by chambers for the senate, and the house—that for the latter being recently constructed. There are also suitable rooms for the different clerks, and offices required by the public business. The chamber for the house of representatives is handsome, but, like some others in more conspicuous places, badly adapted to public speaking.

In the right wing of the building is the office of the adjutant general of Louisiana ; it is also used as a temporary armory, until the law for the erection of a new one is carried into execution. The left room is occupied by offices for the governor, secretary of state, state treasurer, and civil engineer.

The whole was built in 1815. It is in contemplation to erect an edifice more worthy of the state, but when this will be done, or where located, is as yet undetermined. It will probably not be within the precincts of our city, as the late convention provides that the Legislature shall not hold its sessions hereafter within sixty miles of New Orleans. It is doubtless intended that the public servants shall do more work, and less eating, drinking and carousing, than they have heretofore done.

THE CATHEDRAL,

Or *Church of St. Louis*, is the principal and centre of three buildings which stand on Chartres street, immediately opposite to the *Place d'Armes*, or Parade Ground. This edifice forcibly strikes the stranger by its venerable and antique appearance. There is perhaps, none in the Union which is on this account more impressive. The foundation of the building was laid in 1792, and it was, to a certain extent, completed in 1794, at the expense of Don Andre Almonaster, perpetual regidor, and Alvarez Real.

The architecture of the Cathedral is by no means pure, but is not wanting in effect on this account. The lower story is of the rustic order, flanked at each of the front angles by hexagonal towers, projecting one half of their diameter, showing below Tuscan antes at each angle, and above pilasters of plain mason-work, in the same style, with antique wreaths on the frieze of the entablatures. These towers are crowned by low spires, erected after Latrobe's designs, about 1814.

The grand entrance to the Cathedral is in the middle of the front, being a semicircular arched door, with two clustered Tuscan columns on either side. This entrance is flanked by two smaller doors, similar to the principal one.

The second story of the front has the same general appearance, as to the number of columns &c. as the lower one, but is of the Roman Doric order. Above, and corresponding to the main entrance, is a circular window, with niches on either side, above the flanking doors below. On the apex of the pediment of this story rises the chief turret, being in the Tuscan style, and in two parts —the lower being square, about twenty feet in height, with circular apertures on each side ; the upper hexagonal, having a belfry, with apertures at the sides for letting out the sound, flanked by antes. The proportions of the order are not observed in this belfry, which was erected about 1824, by Le Riche.

The Cathedral has a tenure, to speak in legal phrase, of every Saturday evening offering masses for the soul of its founder, Don Andre. The requirement is faithfully observed, for as the day returns, at set of sun, the mournful sound of the tolling bell recalls the memory of the departed. This building is almost inseparably connected, in the minds of the old residents, with the memory of the venerable Pere Antonio de Sedella, curate of the parish for nearly fifty years. This excellent old man, adored for his universal benevolence, came to Louisiana, then a province, in 1779, and is supposed to have performed nearly one half of the marriage and funeral ceremonies of its inhabitants, until the period of his death, at the ripe age of nearly ninety years, in 1837. This venerated relic of by gone days lies burried at the foot of the altar.

ST. PATRICK'S CHURCH,

Is situated in Camp-street, near Lafayette square. The design is a triumph worthy of the genius of Gothic architecture, whether the dimensions, or the splendor of the structure be considered.

The measurement is 93 feet by 164 on the ground ; and from the side walk to the summit of the tower, 190. The style is taken from the famous York Minster Cathedral, and executed agreeably to the designs of Messrs. Dakin & Dakin, which were adopted by the trustees of the church. It surpasses every attempt at a similar order on this side of the Atlantic, and when completed, may proudly challenge comparison with any modern parochial edifice in Europe. It cost about $100,000.

ST. AUGUSTINE CHURCH.

THIS structure, erected in 1841, stands on St. Claude street, corner of Bayou road. It is about 50 feet front by 90 deep. The architect, Mr. Depouilly, has displayed an excellent taste in its construction. The style is of a mixed order, but extremely neat—and in such good keeping, that the interior has the appearance of being much smaller than it actually measures. The decorations are worthy of the sacredness of the place. The colored glass of the windows throws a beautiful mellowed light across the aisles, producing a chastened effect suited to the solemnity of the place. Immediately over the altar is a full length painting of the tutelar saint, which is executed with the bold hand of a master. At the right of this is the Virgin Mary, little inferior to the first, but finished with much greater delicacy of touch. Our Saviour is conspicuously represented in the ceiling, over the centre—around which, on the gallery below, and between the windows, are portraits of the saints, arranged in the pannelwork. Take this church altogether, it is one of the neatest houses of devotion in this city.

ST. ANTOINE'S, OR THE MORTUARY CHAPEL.

On account of the great increase in the population of the city, and consequent greater number of interments, objection was made, about the
year 1822, to the performance of services for the
dead in the Cathedral, it being in a very prominent and public situation. Under these circumstances, the city made a grant of a piece of land
at the corner of Conti and Rampart streets, to the
foundation of the Church of St. Louis, on condition
of their erecting upon the same, a chapel, as a place
for the performance of the funeral ceremonies,
in conformity to the catholic ritual. In pursuance
of this intention, a cross, marking the present site
of the altar of the chapel, was placed there with
proper ceremonies, on the 10th of October, 1826,
and on the following morning the building was begun. Its erection was prosecuted at the expense
of the catholic foundation, and completed within a
year after its commencement, at a cost of about
$16,000.

It is a plain but very neat edifice, of the Gothic
composite order; and was dedicated to the most
holy St. Antony of Padua, as its guardian. All
funeral ceremonies of catholics are performed
there.

5

THE CHAPEL OF THE URSULINES.

An edifice strongly characteristic of our city, and well calculated to cause reflection on the many and sudden changes of dynasty to which New Orleans has been subjected. This building, of a quaint old style of architecture, was erected, according to a Spanish inscription on a marble tablet in the middle of the façade, in 1787, during the reign of Carlos III, (Don Estevan Miro being governor of the province,) by Don Andre Almonaster Y Roxas. It is exceedingly plain and unpretending in its exterior, and chiefly interesting from its associations, and extremely antiquated appearance.

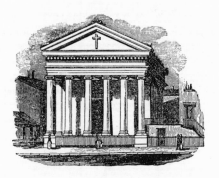

CHRIST CHURCH, (EPISCOPAL.)

A fine Ionic building, situated on Canal, at the corner of Bourbon street, was designed by Gallier and Dakin, architects, and its erection begun in the autumn of 1835, under the direction of Mr. D. H. Toogood. It was completed in the summer of 1837, and consecrated during the same year. The cost of the edifice was about $70,000. The form of the ceiling, being a flat dome, is much admired. The Rev. Dr. Hawkes is pastor of this church.

ST. PAUL'S CHURCH, (EPISCOPAL.)

This is a neat frame structure, located on the corner of Camp and Bartholomew streets. The Rev. Mr. Goodrich officiates in this church.

THE ANNUNCIATION CHURCH, (EPISCOPAL,)

Is to occupy a conspicious place near Annunciation Square. The location was selected with
good taste, both in regard to the beauty of the
position, and to the great improvements of the
neighbourhood. The church is to be placed under the pastoral charge of the Rev. Mr Prescot.

THE FIRST PRESBYTERIAN CHURCH,

Is an edifice of the Grecian Doric order, finely
situated, fronting on Lafayette square—the handsomest public ground in the city. The basement
story is of granite ; the superstructure being

brick, plastered to imitate stone. The building was commenced in November, 1834, and opened for public worship in July, of the following year. It was finished by subscription, at a cost of $55,000. In 1844, this building was considerably enlarged. In the court, in front, a neat obelisk has been erected, as a monument to the memory of the Rev. Sylvester Larned, first Presbyterian pastor of this city, who died 31st August, 1820, at the early age of 24, much and deservedly regretted. Rev. Mr Scott, is the present pastor.

THE SECOND PRESBYTERIAN CHURCH.

This is a plain and unpretending structure, on the corner of Calliope and Phytanee streets ; and like its near neighbour, St. Paul's, evidently erected more for utility than for external display. It is a neat frame building, with only sufficient ornament to give to it the appearance of a place of public worship. Rev. Mr. Stanton is the pastor.

THE FIRST CONGREGATIONAL CHURCH,

Is an edifice of brick, in the plain Gothic style of architecture. It was erected in 1817, on St. Charles street at the corner of Gravier, where formerly stood the store-houses of the Jesuits, and upon a part of the foundations of those buildings. Rev. Mr Clapp, is the pastor.

THE METHODIST EPISCOPAL CHURCH,

At the corner of Poydras and Carondolet streets, is of the Grecian Doric order, the details of which are copied from the temple of Theseus, at Athens. The height of the steeple is 170 feet from the side walk. This edifice was erected in the year 1836—7, by Messrs. Dakin, and Dakin, architects, at an expense of $50,000. Rev. Mr Nicholson officiating as pastor.

THE FIRST BAPTIST CHURCH,

Is under the pastoral care of Rev. Mr. Hinton.

WESLEYAN CHAPEL.

This is a plain frame building, on St. Paul near Poydras street, and is devoted to the colored portion of the community.

THE OLD URSULINE CONVENT,

Situated in Conde street, was completed by the French government, in 1733; and is therefore, probably, the most ancient edifice in Louisiana. The architecture is plain, being Tuscan composite, and the smallness of the windows, and the peculiar form of the roof and chimnies, together with the general venerable and time worn aspect of the building, render it, independent of its history, an object of interest to both citizens and strangers.

It was occupied by the Ursuline nuns for nearly a century; and only abandoned by them, when, on account of the great rise in the value of real estate around it, they disposed of a part of their property, and removed, in 1824, to the new convent, two miles below the city. It was then used by the state legislature, as a place for their sessions, until their present accommodations were prepared for their reception, in 1834. Since that period it has been inhabited by the Right Rev. Bishop Blanc, and several other of the higher clergy of the diocess. From its great solidity of construction, there is no reason to doubt but that it may stand many years longer, as a monument of "the olden times."

THE NEW CONVENT.

This richly endowed establishment was founded in 1826, and the chapel was completed in 1829. The main building is about 100 feet long, of brick, two stories high, and has two wings, running from the rear, at each end. It is principally occupied as a seminary for the education of young ladies. The average price for instruction and board is $200 per annum. The number of scholars at present is 120. On a line with this building is the nunnery, containing 40 sisters of the Ursuline order. Annexed to the latter edifice is the chapel, a remarkably neat and plain structure. Immediately in front of the latter building is the residence of the priests. There are eighty acres of land, three of which are enclosed and beautifully embellished. The position is pleasant and healthy. It fronts upon the river, two miles below the city, and embraces a charming view of the Mississippi.

THE CARMELITE CONVENT,

Is a frame building, which stands upon ground adjoining the church of St. Augustine, and is occupied by the nuns of this order. They have an excellent school under their care, divided into two apartments—one of which is appropriated to white and the other to free colored children, many of the latter class, have wealthy parents, and pay a high price for their education.

THE CYPRESS GROVE CEMETERY.

This resting place for the dead is about four miles from the centre of the city upon the right of the upper Shell Road, that leads to lake Pontchartrain, and occupies a ridge, which is supposed once to have been the embankment of the Mississippi.

The plat of ground devoted to the cemetery, measures 244 by 2700 feet. The spot was purchased and improved at an expense of $35,000, by the Firemen's Charitable Association. The revenue that arises from interments is exclusively devoted to benevolent purposes—all the business of the association being conducted by its members without any compensation. The front wall and lodges are built in pure Egyptian style, and cost

5*

$8,000. The grounds are divided into avenues, and arranged and embellished with an effect appropriate to the solemn associations of the place.

The simple and striking motto over the entrance is selected from Pierpont :—

> " Here to thy bosom, mother earth,
>   Take back in peace, what thou hast given ;
> And, all that is of heavenly birth,
>   O God, in peace recall to heaven."

Some of the tombs are very richly wrought—and, one in particular, erected by a fire company, a memento to a brother who was killed in the performance of his duty, is a specimen of superior skill and workmanship. The nature of the soil admits graves to be sunk six feet without approaching water. They are laid with brick and securely cemented. The tombs above ground (here called *ovens*, which they somewhat resemble) are faced with marble, built in the best manner. There are four hundred of them, which cost an average of twenty-five dollars each. These are sold at fifty dollars, and the surplus goes into the funds of the society, for charitable purposes.

A central avenue, twenty-eight feet in width, called Live Oak Avenue, traverses the whole length of the ground. Cedar and Magnolia avenues, on either side of this, are each twenty feet wide. Next the outer walls, are those named Cypress and Willow, of eighteen feet each. At a distance of every two hundred feet, are transverse avenues. The spaces between these are reserved for the erection of tombs, and may be purchased at a stipulated price, according to the location. These privileges are sold in fee for ever, and the title is held sacred in the eye of the law.

CATHOLIC CEMETERIES.

Of these there are two. The larger ranges between Robertson and Claiborne, and extends from St. Louis to Canal streets, occupying four full squares. The square on St. Louis street is principally appropriated to natives of France and their descendants. There is a great deal of refined sentiment and delicate fancy in some of their memorials of the departed. Tombs are often embellished with fresh flowers, that look as if they received daily attentions. This is a custom not peculiar to the French, but seems to be the natural language of that refined affection, which cherishes the memory and the virtues of the dead, among the dearest and most sacred treasures of the heart. The smaller of these grounds lies on Basin and St. Louis streets. It presents, like the other, many tasteful monuments, that show us where repose the honored and the wealthy of the land These necessarily attract the notice of strangers—but there is one among them less conspicuous than the rest, the eloquence of whose simple and touch-

ing memorial has rarely been surpassed. It is in
the side wall, near the north-west corner of the
cemetery, surrounded by many more of a similar
construction. There is no display—only a simple
record, that tells it is occupied by a female fifteen
years of age. Beneath this is quite a plain stone,
with the inscription "*Ma pauvre fille!*" What
an affecting history in those three brief words!
It was undoubtedly placed there by an affectionate
mother, deploring the untimely death of a beloved
daughter. It contains more pathos, and speaks to
the heart with more effect, than volumes of labored eulogy, or frantic grief. The proud mausole-
um, and the turgid epitaph, sink into insignificance
beside this humble burst of maternal love—"*My
poor child!*"

Illustrative of the false pride with which the
Creole population still, unfortunately, regard the
practice of duelling, nearly opposite is the following inscription:—

> "*Victime de l' honneur.*
>   Aet. 24."

THE PROTESTANT CEMETERY.

This burial place fronts on St. Paul street, and
occupies about two city squares. The inscriptions
do not date back beyond 1810. It is a spot, however, where the northern and eastern traveller
will often recognize familiar names of those who

have found graves far from endeared friends and connexions. There is little of the display here that is observed in other grounds. Tombs that, apparently, were commenced with a resolution to show honor to the departed, have been left without a stone to record the name of the neglected tenant.

In one of the side walls, is a tomb stone of plain white marble, with only the words, "MY HUSBAND!" engraven upon it. In this vault were deposited the remains of a distinguished tragedian, who fell a victim to the yellow fever, some years since, in this city. It is a delicate souvenir, that bespeaks the true feeling and affection of a desolate widow. On another is the emphatic inscription, "*Poor Caroline!*"

ST. PATRICK'S CEMETERY.

Is situated within sight of the Cypress Grove Cemetery, and having been but recently commenced, has not yet become an object of much attraction.

There is quite a spacious Catholic burying ground near Bayou road, more than a mile back of the city, that seems to have been considerably used, but has few monuments of any interest.

Besides these, there is a general burying ground at Lafayette. The Jews have a place of interment, also, in that city.

CHARITABLE INSTITUTIONS.

—

THERE is probably no city in the United States that has so many benevolent institutions as New Orleans, in proportion to its population. Certainly it has not an equal in those voluntary contributions, which are sometimes required to answer the immediate calls of distress. Here are assembled a mixed multitude, composed of almost every nation and tongue, from the frozen to the torrid zone, and, whether it be the sympathy of strangers, or the influence of the sunny south, their purses open and their hearts respond, like those of brothers, to the demands of charity. To illustrate these assertions and to carry out the plan of this work, a description of the most prominent of these establishments is annexed.

THE FEMALE ORPHAN ASYLUM

Stands at the intersection of Camp and Phytanee streets, on an angular lot, widening to the rear on Erato street. It has a northerly front on the junction of the two first named streets, and occupies all the grounds that are contained in this irregular space—the rear, however, being reserved

as a site for a church, to be erected at some future period. The land was a liberal donation from Madame Foucher, and her brother, Francis Soulet. Previous to the erection of this building, the establishment was conducted in rented tenements, under the direction of the Sisters of Charity; in whose hands it still continues to present a praiseworthy example of neatness and parental care. It commenced in 1836 with *six* children; and, in 1839, with great exertions, it accommodated *ninety*.

The history of this charity seems to trespass on the region of romance. In its struggle, it received an important impulse from the suggestions of a benevolent lady, Mrs. Pogue. In conversation with a female friend of similar feelings, she remarked, "if a fair could be organized for its benefit, and the opulent induced to patronize it, money might be raised to erect the necessary buildings." That friend told the Bishop; who, taking up the hint, announced it from the pulpit. This led to the call of a meeting—where, instead of a small assemblage, the rooms were crowded with the wealth and beauty of the city. It result-ed in the collection of over *sixteen thousand dollars!* Thus, to almost a chance expression from the kind heart of woman, New Orleans is mainly in-debted for the prosperity of one of the noblest of her humane institutions.

From this moment, the Asylum assumed a firm standing. A suitable house was at once com-menced. The second municipality gave a thou-sand dollars, and the legislature at different periods, twelve thousand dollars. In 1840 the whole was completed, and the children, to the number of about one hundred, took possession. Since that time they have averaged one hundred and forty-five annually. They receive the rudi-ments of a good education. At a suitable age they are apprenticed to persons of character and responsibility ; and a vigilance is continued, that guaranties to them the kind treatment, which their isolated position seems to demand.

The edifice, built by D. Hayden, cost over forty-two thousand dollars. Though conducted *with the utmost prudence*, the institution is some twenty-five hundred dollars in debt. In a capital like this, where so many of the citizens have princely revenues, and with them a princely liberality, there is little doubt that arrangements will soon be made to relieve it of this embarrassment. It has now about one hundred and sixty children, of whom over thirty are in the nursery.

THE MALE ORPHAN ASYLUM.

The Society for the Relief of Destitute Orphan Boys have their establishment in Lafayette. It went into operation in 1824, and was incorporated the year after. By a calculation of the first sixteen years, it appears that an average of thirty-five have annually participated in its benefits. Although its title would seem to imply, that orphans only are admitted, yet the board are authorized to receive any boy, whose destitute condition requires their protection.

THE POYDRAS FEMALE ORPHAN ASYLUM.

This is one of the oldest establisments of the kind in New Orleans. It was endowed by Julien Poydras, and possesses an immense revenue from valuable improved real estate. They occupy on Julia, from St. Charles to Carondelet streets, and extend back about two-thirds of an immense square. It has for several years had an average of one hundred and twenty children. The excellent system and regulations, in regard both to instruction and health, will not be disparaged by comparison with the best institutions in the world. Possessing so much property and such beautiful grounds, it is to be regretted that more spacious and comfortable buildings are not erected for the accommodation of the inmates.

THE CATHOLIC MALE ORPHAN ASYLUM.

This institution is supported by an association, and by private donations. The establishment occupies a large building fronting the river, and a few squares above the New Convent. About one hundred and seventy children receive the benefits of this charity.

LES DAMES DE LA PROVIDENCE.

This association was formed in 1839. It consists of about one hundred ladies, who each contribute a certain sum monthly as a charitable fund. Its object is to render aid to the sick, the poor and the infirm. The institution was put into operation by the benevolent French ladies of New Orleans; and, were its resources equal to the kind feelings of its members, it would be rendered a means of alleviating much distress among the sick and destitute.

THE SAMARITAN CHARITABLE ASSOCIATION.

This institution was founded during the epidemic of 1837, for the purpose of alleviating the wants of the poor and the sick. They established an office at that period, where some of the members, day and night, were always in readiness to attend the bed-side of disease, and to administer aid to the indigent. The late mayor, and many of the most wealthy citizens are members ; and, in time of need, the association is liberally endowed by the spontaneous donations of the generous public.

THE FIREMEN'S CHARITABLE ASSOCIATION

Was incorporated in 1835, and managed by a board of directors chosen from each company, subject to certain restrictions. The officers, (a president, vice president, secretary and treasurer,) are elected by the board from members of the association, on the first Monday of January, of each year. The object of this society is the relief of its members, who are incapacitated from attending to business from sickness or misfortunes not arising from improper causes. It makes provision also for the benefit of their families—particularly widows and orphans. This is a very laudable association, and every way deserving of the excellent fire department from which it originated.

YOUNG MEN'S HOWARD ASSOCIATION.

This benevolent institution was established in 1837 ; and its object is the relief of the indigent and sick. Its resources depend entirely upon public contributions—and appeals for aid have always been responded to with alacrity. During the prevalence of the epidemic of 1841, this society collected and distributed over five thousand dollars among the sufferers on that dreadful occasion. It is a noble charity that waits not for calls upon its benevolence; but its members seek for worthy objects in the hidden recesses of misery, and soothe and administer to their wants, with a brotherly solicitude that does honor to the name they have assumed.

THE HEBREW BENEVOLENT SOCIETY,

Although but a short time in existence, has accomplished much good; diffusing charity, not in mere accordance with sectional prejudices, but in that catholic spirit of genuine benevolence, which freely dispenses its benefits alike upon Jew and Christian, and recognizes but one brotherhood in the family of man.

THE MILNE ORPHAN ASYLUM.

This institution was endowed in 1839, by Alexander Milne, a liberal Scotch gentleman, from whom it takes its name. It was established for the education and protection of helpless orphan children of both sexes.

HOSPITALS.

No city in the United States is so well provided
with establishments of this kind as New Orleans.
Here, the only passport required for admission to
the best attendance, is sickness, or an injury.
No cold formalities are thrown in the way of the
suffering patient. Indeed, it has become a subject
of complaint, that access is so easy, and the position so agreeable, that the improvident and the in-
dolent take undue advantage of its benefits.

THE CHARITY HOSPITAL.

The first hospital for indigent persons erected
in the city of New Orleans, appears to have been

built on the site formed by the west side of Rampart street, between Toulouse and St. Peter streets. It was blown down in 1779; and, being of wood, was entirely destroyed.

In 1784, Dr. N. Y. Roxas commenced one of brick on the same position, which he completed at an expense of $114,000 in 1786, and called it the New Charity Hospital of St. Charles. He endowed it with a perpetual revenue of $1500 per annum, by appropriating the rents of the stores at the corner of St. Peter and Levee streets. It continued under the patronage and direction of the family, until March 1811, when it was relinquished to the city by authority of the legislature, the edifice having been previously consumed by fire. It was now subjected to a council of administration, appointed by the governor and city council—(the first six, the latter three.) Since 1813 the council has been appointed by the governor and senate. It consists of eight members, and the governor. Its support has been derived from several sources. A most liberal legacy was left it by that public benefactor Julien Poydras, of real estate, valued at $35,000. Several smaller sums have been received from other benevolent individuals. It has also received aid from the state, directly and indirectly. Pennsylvania made a liberal grant of $10,000, in 18—.

In 1812, the council of administration sold to

the state the square now occupied by the state house, with the buildings, for $125,000, and purchased the present site, and built their large and commodious structure at the foot of Common street, at an expense of $150,000, containing sufficient room to accommodate four or five hundred patients. This is the building particularly referred to in the heading of this article. Besides being under the charge of the ablest of the medical faculty, the institution has the assistance of the Sisters of Charity, as nurses to the sick, who cannot be excelled in kindness and careful attention.

The edifice itself is very imposing, from its immense size. It is substantially built with brick. Suitable supplementary out-buildings for lunatics, and lying-in apartments, are on the same grounds; and the whole is encompassed by a permanent brick wall.

To show the great usefulness of this establishment, it is only necessary to state that, during 1844, there were five thousand eight hundred and forty-six patients admitted, seven hundred and thirteen of whom died, and five thousand and fifty-nine were dismissed. Of this number, only one thousand three hundred and sixteen were natives of the United States, and four thousand five hundred and thirty foreigners. This year the yellow fever was not epidemic.

The following table, taken from the New Orleans Medical Journal, shows the number of cases of yellow fever admitted into this hospital from Jan. 1, 1822, to Jan. 1, 1844, with the dates of the first and last cases each year, with the discharges and deaths, constituting a term of twenty-two years.

TABLE.

Year.	First Case.	Last Case.	Adm'd	Dis'g'd	Died.
1822	Sept. 3.	Dec. 31.	349	98	239
1823	Sept. 11.		1		1
1824	Aug. 4.	Nov. 13.	167	59	108
1825	June 23.	Dec. 19.	94	40	59
1826	May 18.	Nov. 18.	26	19	5
1827	July 17.	Dec. 5.	372	263	109
1828	June 19.	Dec. 10.	290	160	130
1829	May 23.	Nov. 29.	435	220	215
1830	July 24.	Nov. 29.	256	139	117
1831	June 9.	Oct. 7.	3	1	2
1832	Aug. 15.	Oct. 25.	26	8	18
1833	July 17.	Nov. 17.	422	212	210
1834	Aug. 28.	Nov. 22.	150	55	95
1835	Aug. 24.	Nov. 27.	505	221	284
1836	Aug. 24.	Oct. 25.	6	1	5
1837	July 13.	Nov. 17.	998	556	442
1838	Aug. 25.	Nov. 1.	22	5	17
1839	July 23.	Nov. 17.	1086	634	452
1840	July 9.		3		3
1841	Aug. 2.	Dec. 8.	1113	520	594
1842	Aug. 4.	Nov. 26.	410	214	211
1843	July 10.	Dec. 31.	1053	609	487
Total Number, : : : :			7787	4034	3803
A discrepancy of : : :			50		4034
			7837		7837

" This discrepancy between the number of ad-
mittances, discharges, and deaths," say the editors,
"arises from the fact that a good many cases of
yellow fever occur, after the patients are admitted
into the hospital for other diseases—and some
remain to be treated for other diseases, long after
having been cured of yellow fever ; and, it may
be, that some cases are not noted upon the hospital
books at all." The proportion of deaths is ac-
counted for by the exposed state of the patient
before admission. In private practice they do not
average one death to ten.

The absence of quarantine regulations in New
Orleans, is often remarked by strangers. Acts
of legislation have been passed at different times,
establishing laws for the protection of the city,
which proved of but little service, owing, it is generally admitted, to their not being carried out as
it is now known they should have been to test their
efficacy, consequently they soon fell into disuse.

Much able, and it would seem unanswerable
argument has been employed, to prove that this
scourge of tropical climates is not contagious ; yet,
Dr. Carpenter, an eminent and learned member of
the medical profession of this city, with great research, has tracked it through all its secret channels of communication, by which at different periods it has been introduced.

The recent able essay of Dr. Hort, read before

6

the Physico-Medical Society of this city, and the proceedings and resolutions of that body, had in reference to it, with equal conclusiveness show it to be endemic, or of local origin, and not an imported or contagious disease.

When such eminent "doctors disagree" what shall the unlearned and uninitiated do?—we are surely in a dilemma, and hardly know on which horn to hang our own humble judgment—but it would really appear that with a sanitary system, commending itself to the more cautious views of the Atlantic cities, an advantage would be gained, that would far more than balance any diminished trade of our neighbors in the Gulf. Are there not also, many hundreds of active, intelligent, business making citizens, who now fly to the North on the first approach of the sickly season, who, with such guards faithfully maintained about them, would remain through the summer? and are there not thousands more in various parts of the country, who, inspired with confidence by the existence and maintenance of a system of measures which *they* deem essential to the preservation of the health and lives of the citizens, would throng to our metropolis as the most inviting field of enterprize, and thus multiply our numbers and enlarge our business far more rapidly than it can, or will be done under the present system?

If in making these suggestions it should be sup-

posed that we have "defined our position," we
shall shelter ourselves under "the generally received opinion" "the prevailing fears of the community"—and the prudential measures of other
cities.

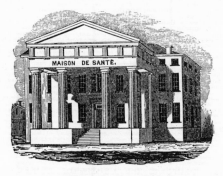

MAISON DE SANTE.

This noble edifice, emphatically the house of
the stranger, was built in 1839, and opened in Au-
gust of the same year. The full and complete
success of the enterprise is written in the grateful
memories of the thousands of patients who have
resorted to it in the hour of sickness and danger.
The prices required secure to every sick person
more than the attention and comforts of the house
of his childhood. Not a doubt need to cross his
mind but that all which science, and the most devoted care can effect, will be done for him; he

only goes there to get well, if it be possible in the nature of his case. The names of the attending physicians, Doctors Stone, Kennedy and Carpenter, are a sufficient guaranty for the respectability of this establishment.

CIRCUS STREET INFIRMARY.

This institution, situated between Poydras and Perdido streets, was established by Doctors Campbell and Mackie, in July, 1841. It is neatly furnished, and offers all the comforts and advantages of a private house to the invalid. No contagious diseases are admitted, and kind and skilful nurses are furnished.

THE FRANKLIN INFIRMARY,

Is situated in the Fauxbourg Franklin, in Champs Elysees street, fronting the Pontchartrain rail-road, and about two miles from the city. It is a private hospital, founded by Dr. C. A. Luzemburg. The building, although not large, is accommodated with several out houses, and the grounds are spacious and pleasant.

THE UNITED STATES MARINE HOSPITAL,

Situated at Macdonough, opposite New Orleans, occupies a square, measuring three hundred and fifty feet each way, which is enclosed by a good substantial fence, intended, eventually, to give place to an iron railing. The edifice measures, in front, one hundred and sixty feet, by seventy eight deep—from the rear of which two adjuncts extend fifty feet further back, leaving sufficient room between them for a spacious court, immediately behind the centre of the main building.

The whole is laid off into three stories. It is fifty feet from the ground to the eaves, and one hundred and thirty-five to the top of the flag-staff, which surmounts the belvidere. It is built in the Gothic style; and was designed by Mondele and Reynolds, who were the original contractors. It was commenced in 1834, but for want of the necessary appropriations by the government, the work was suspended, and has gone so much to ruin, that it will require $20,000 to repair the damage.

James H. Caldwell, Esq., has contracted for the completion of this work. The building, when finished and furnished for receiving patients, will cost $130,000. It will accommodate two hundred and sixty nine persons. The grounds, tastefully laid out, are to be embellished with shrubbery. As seen from the Mississippi, or from a distance, this structure presents a very majestic appearance. It stands in a healthy position, elevated and dry; and from its great height, commands a complete view of the river, city, surrounding country, and a whole forest of masts—affording to poor Jack at at once a delightful and a busy prospect, that must have a great tendency to cheer the hours of his convalescence.

PUBLIC BUILDINGS.

—

THE MUNICIPAL HALL.

This edifice, when completed, will be one of
the noblest public buildings of the Second Municipality. It is to occupy the corner of Hevia and
St. Charles streets, facing the westerly side of
Lafayette Square, a site selected particularly on
account of its conspicuous and airy position. Its
grand entrance ranges along the latter thorough-
fare 90 feet, running back upon the former 208,

and presenting an altitude of 54 feet to the eaves, displaying two bold stories above a basement of 11 feet ceiling. This lower apartment is intended for the accommodation of the military, and the police and watch departments. It is intersected from end to end by a corridor twelve, and across, in the centre, by one of fourteen feet wide, the latter giving room for a double flight of stairs, which ascend to the upper story. The same division of passage-ways is observed on each floor.

The grand entrance from St. Charles street, is by a flight of eighteen blue Quincy-granite steps, of which material the principal front is constructed. At the top of these, at an elevation of fourteen feet, is a platform extending along the whole front, twenty-five feet deep, sustaining, by a range of six pillars in front, and four in the rear, a massy pediment, all of which is of Ionic Grecian construction, and in good keeping with the main fabric. On entering the corridor through this portico, on the right hand, is an apartment seventy-five by thirty-five feet, and, and like all the others on this floor, eighteen feet in the ceiling, appropriated to the library of the School Lyceum. In the rear of this, on the same side, are four others for public offices and courts, as are also those on the opposite direction.

Ascending to the third story, in front is the great hall, sixty-one by eighty-four feet, and twenty-

nine in the ceiling, set apart for the School Lyceum. Immediately in front of this, is a central
platform, advancing between two side rooms, over
which are two others, similar, all four of which
are intended for the accommodation of the apparatus, necessary for this new institution.

The main room is furnished with galleries on
three sides, arranged in the best manner for the
convenience of scholars and spectators. The
rooms in the rear, like those in the story below,
are devoted to public offices.

The walls of this building are to be based upon
granite, and the residue of white marble, after the
Grecian Ionic order. The whole will cost about
$120,000.

THE CITY PRISONS.

These edifices are built of brick, and plastered
to imitate granite, they are three stories in height,
occupying one hundred and twenty three feet on
Orleans and St. Ann streets, by one hundred and
thirty-eight feet nine inches between them. They
are two in number, and divided by a passage way
that is closed to the public. The principal building has its main entrance from Orleans street,
through a circular vestibule, closed by strong iron
doors. The lower story contains the offices and
apartments of the jailor. The second story is divided into large halls for such prisoners as require

6*

to be less strictly guarded. The plan of the third
story is similar. The whole is surmounted by a
belvidere, with an alarm bell. The cost is estimated at $200,000.

SECOND MUNICIPALITY WORK-HOUSE.

This institution was formed in obedience to legislative enactment, under date of the 5th of March,
1841. The buildings were completed and occupied the same year. The site is a portion detached
from the northern extremity of the Protestant
Episcopal Burying Ground, and the centre of the
front is directly facing St. Mary street. The plot
is two hundred and ninety feet, front and rear,
and two hundred and fifty-five deep—the whole
being enclosed by a wall twenty-one feet high,
twenty-six inches thick at the base, and eighteen
at the top, externally supported throughout by
abutments at a distance of every fourteen feet.

The entrance is by a strong and well secured
gate, into a public passage flanked by offices,
over which are rooms assigned to the use of the
keepers, for the accommodation of the guard, and
such *materiel* as good order, and the safety of the
establishment require. This structure is partially
separated from the prison by well constructed
gates and partition walls. Within, on each side,
engrossing the residue of the immediate front of
the grounds, are two buildings. The one on the

right is for white females, and that on the left for blacks of both sexes. These tenements are divided from the other parts of the prison by high fences of frame work. Going thence into the principal yard, the building for the male whites is seen on the extreme right. This is of one story, measuring eighty by thirty feet, and is the largest one on the premises. Arranged along near the rear wall, extending to the left, are the work shops.

The average number of white prisoners is eighty, not one-seventh of whom are females; and one hundred blacks, a third of these also being females. The prison discipline seems to be of a first rate order; and it is seldom necessary to punish for offences against the rules. Religious service is performed on Sundays, and a physician is in attendance every day. It is a singular fact, that only five persons have died there since it was opened, notwithstanding their former irregular habits. The prisoners are kept at constant labor; and their food, though not luxurious, is of a wholesome nature, which may, when their abstinence from intemperate habits is taken into consideration, account for the excellent state of their health. It would not be hazarding much to say that many here were never before accustomed to so many of the comforts of life—"in all, save these bonds;" for they lodge upon clean and comfortable bedding, surrounded by moscheto bars; and, once a week, at least, can enjoy the luxury of a bath.

This is the receptacle of that class of society, both white and black, who are denominated vagrants. They embrace two sorts of individuals—those who have no visible means of obtaining a livelihood, and those who live by committing unlawful depredations upon others. Besides these, colored seamen, while in port, not being suffered by the laws to go at large, are accommodated, for the time being, with an apartment in the Workhouse. Slaves are placed here by their masters, for punishment, for safe keeping, and for refusing to perform labor, as well as for the commission of crimes. These last are sent out in gangs, under keepers, to clean the streets, and to perform certain other menial services within the control of the municipal authorities.

Nothing could render this establishment more complete, except a classification of its inmates; so that the hardened offenders should be prevented from drawing the young, the thoughtless, and the incipient transgressor, into the vortex of their own viciousness. To the philanthropist, this must be a consideration of the utmost importance. The saying, that "evil communications corrupt good manners," is illustrated even in this place—and here, many who seem upon the very verge of destruction, might be saved from ultimate and utter ruin, by the judicious care and protection of the humane and reflecting magistrate.

THIRD MUNICIPALITY WORK-HOUSE.

This new establishment stands on Moreau street, running from Louisa to Piety streets, and taking within its limits the building formerly used as the Washington market, which has been altered to suit its present purpose. The buildings were prepared under the superintendence of Charles K. Wise, and are well arranged. The prisoners average about one hundred—thirty of whom are females. The regulations are excellent.

THE COURT-HOUSE.

This edifice stands on Chartres street, and to the right of the Cathedral, as it is seen from the Place d'Armes, opposite to which it is situated. The lower story is of the Tuscan order, with a wide portico along the front of the edifice, supported by ten antes, between semi-circular arches. The four in the middle are strengthened in front by Tuscan columns, and those at the angles by two clustered pilastres. The ascent to the second story is through the principal entrance, which is composed of a semi-circular arched door, with antes at the sides, and Doric entablature. It opens into a spacious lobby, through which, by a stone stair-way, of a single flight below, and a

double one above, the second floor is reached.
The front of the upper story is of the Ionic order,
but generally similar to the lower.   The entablature is surmounted by a denticulated cornice, and
the pediment is relieved by an oblong shield.

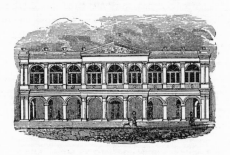

THE CITY HALL.

This building stands on the upper side of the
Cathedral, on a line with the Court House described above, both of which were erected the latter
part of the preceding century, through the liberality of Don Andre Almonester.   This edifice in all
general respects, much resembles the Court-
House on the right of the Cathedral, except that
the main entrance, under the portico, is of the
Tuscan order; and that the stair within is a
winding one, leading to the upper story by three
flights ; also, that the pediment of the front bears
the American eagle, with cannon and piles of balls.

MARKETS.

The markets are a prominent feature in a description of New Orleans. They are numerous, and dispersed, to suit the convenience of the citizens. The prices of many articles they offer are very fluctuating. Not dearer, however, on an average, than in New York. Stall-fatted meats are not so usual here as at the North, preference being given to the grass-fed. The mutton has no equal in America. Poultry and fish are fine; and vegetables, except potatoes, are abundant, and speak well for the soil that produced them. Fruit, from the West Indies and our own West, is not only plenty, but of the best kind. The regulations are excellent, and are strictly enforced by officers appointed for that purpose.

The greatest market day is Sunday, during the morning. At break of day the gathering commences—youth and age, beauty and the not-so-beautiful—all colors, nations and tongues are commingled in one heterogeneous mass of delightful confusion; and, he must be a stranger indeed, who elbows his way through the dense crowd, without hearing the welcome music of his own native language. The traveller, who leaves the city without visiting one of the popular markets on Sunday morning, has suffered a rare treat to escape him. Annexed is a brief descriptive account of them.

POYDRAS STREET MARKET,

Is designed for the accommodation of the inhabitants in the rear portion of the second municipality. It covers a space of ground in Poydras street forty-two feet wide by four hundred and two long —extending from near Baronne to Circus street. It was built in 1837, and cost $40,000.

THE VEGETABLE MARKET.

The ground plan of this building is irregular; having been constructed at different periods. It approaches the Roman Doric order—is supported by brick columns plastered, and covered with a wooden frame roof tiled. It fronts on Old Levee, St. Philip and Ursuline streets, and the river. The design was by J. Pilié, who superintended the work. It was completed in 1830, at an expense of $25,800.

THE MEAT MARKET.

Built in the rusticated Doric order, was completed in 1813, after the designs of J. Piernas, city surveyor. The building is of brick plastered, with a wooden frame roof, covered with slate. It is situated on the Levee, and extends from St. Ann to Main streets; and, from its favorable location, and neat simplicity of architecture, is a striking object to those who approach the city by water. It cost about $30,000.

ST. MARY'S MARKET.

This building fronts on Tchoupitoulas street, and runs to New Levee, a distance of four hundred and eighty-six feet by a width of forty-two feet. It was completed in 1836, in the rusticated Doric order, at a cost of about $48,000. In the vicinity, on the first named street, is a vegetable market—a very neat edifice.

———

Besides these, there is a very respectable market at the head of Elysian Fields street, near the Levee; and another in Orleans, between Marais and Villeré streets, near the City Prison.

EXCHANGE HOTEL, (ST. CHARLES.)

This magnificent establishment, which, for size and architectural beauty, stands unrivalled, was commenced in the summer of 1835, and finished in the May of 1838, by an incorporated company. The building was designed by, and erected under

the superintendence of J. Gallier, architect, at an
expense of $600,000, including the ground it stands
on, which cost $100,000. It presents fronts on three
streets.   The principal one on St. Charles street,
consists of a projecting portico of six Corinthian
columns, which stand upon a granite basement
fourteen feet high, with a pediment on the top, and
four similar columns on each side of the portico,
placed in a range with the front wall; behind
which is formed a recess fifteen feet wide and one
hundred and thirty-nine long, and floored over
with large granite slabs, which, supported on iron
beams, serve as a ceiling to that portion of the
basement story standing under the portico; and on
top affords a delightful promenade under the shade
of the portico and side columns.   The entrance
to the bar-room is under this; and the outside

steps, leading from the street to the portico, are placed on each side thereof, between it and the front range of the building. In one of the rear angles of the basement is a bathing establishment, consisting of fourteen rooms, elegantly fitted up, with every convenience for hot or cold bathing. On the opposite angle are placed the wine cellars, store-house, and other domestic apartments. All the remaining parts of the basement are divided into stores, which are rented out to various trades-people. The bar room is in the basement, near the centre of the edifice ; and is octangular in the plan, seventy feet in diameter, and twenty high ; having an interior circular range of Ionic columns, distributed so as to support the weight of the floors and partitions of the upper stories. The architecture of this room is Ionic. That of the saloon, which is immediately over the bar room, is of the Corinthian order, and eighteen feet ceiling. A grand spiral stair-case commences upon the centre of the saloon floor, and is continued up to the dome. Around this stair-case, on each side of the upper stories, a gallery is formed, which gives access to six bedrooms within the octagon, on each of the six upper stories. As the bar room is six feet higher than the other parts of the basement, the entrance to the saloon from the portico is by a flight of marble steps, twelve in number, and thirty-five feet long. On the top of these steps is placed a beautiful marble statue of Washington, presented to the company by John Hagan, Esq.

The gentlemen's dining and sitting rooms occupy the whole side of the building on Gravier street. The dining room, with a pantry at the end, is one hundred and twenty-nine feet long by fifty wide, and twenty-two feet high, tastefully finished in the Corinthian order, with two inside ranges of columns, so placed that there is abundant space for four ranges of dining tables, sufficient to accommodate five hundred persons. The ladies' dining room is placed over the bathing apartments, and is fifty-two by thirty-six feet. The kitchen, fifty-eight by twenty-nine feet, is placed in the rear wing of the building, on the same story with, and in the centre between the two dining rooms. The two angles of the principal front contain the ladies' drawing room, and the gentlemen's sitting room, the former forty by thirty-two feet, the latter thirty-eight feet square. There are nine private parlors on the second story, to some of which are attached adjoining bedrooms; and the same number on the upper stories. There are four stories of elegantly furnished and well lighted bedrooms, all around the four sides of the building, with central passages, or corridors, which communicate with the centre and with each other, having three stair-cases opening to the corridors, besides the grand stair-case in the octagon. There are, in the edifice, three hundred and fifty rooms.

A dome, of beautiful proportions, after a plan of Dakin, forty-six feet in diameter, surmounts the octagon building, elevated upon an order of fluted columns, which stand eleven feet from the dome, around the outside, and on the dome is elevated an elegant little Corinthian turret.   There is a large circular room under the dome, on the floor of which the spiral stair-case terminates, and around the outside of which the circular colonade forms a beautiful gallery eleven feet wide, from whence can be seen the whole city, and all the windings of the river for several miles in each direction. The effect of the dome upon the sight of the visitor, as he approaches the city, is similar to that of St. Paul's, London.

No better evidence can be adduced—nor more flattering encomiums presented to the architects, than the fact of the indescribable effect of the sublime and matchless proportions of this building upon all spectators—even the stoical Indian and the cold and strange backwoodsman, when they first view it, are struck with wonder and delight.   The view of this structure by moonlight is a sight not easily described.   The furnishing of this establishment cost $150,000.

THE VERANDAH,

So called from being covered on its front toward the streets, to a certain height, by a projecting roof

and balcony, is situated at the corner of St. Charles and Common streets, diagonally opposite the Exchange Hotel. The building was intended for a family hotel, by its enterprising projector and builder, the late R. O. Pritchard.

The great dining room, is, probably, one of the most highly finished apartments in America. The ceiling, especially, is a model; being composed of three elliptic domes for chandeliers. This room measures eighty-five by thirty-two feet, and twenty-seven high. The chimney pieces of the ladies' parlors are fine specimens of sculpture, and the rooms are otherwise handsome. The sleeping apartments are not excelled. The whole was designed and constructed by Dakin & Dakin, architects, in 1836–8, at a cost of $300,000, including the ground.

ST. LOUIS HOTEL.

This building, as a hotel, may be considered as one of the most respectable in New Orleans. It stands nearly in the centre of the French portion of the population; and, in the combination of its brilliant and business-like appearance, is not an inappropriate representative of their national character. In this establishment the *utile et dulci* are so happily blended, that the accomplished guest can find no cause of complaint. A more particular description of this superb edifice is omitted here, in consequence of its being given under the head of the City Exchange, to which the reader is respectfully referred.

HEWLETT'S HOTEL.

This is a large and well-constructed building, on the corner of Camp and Common streets. It has been long known as a hotel, but, during the last year, has been opened, under new auspices, by the gentleman whose name has become associated with that of the house. The position is airy, healthy and central, and the table is said to be unexcelled.

———

The Planter's Hotel, in Canal street, and the National Hotel, in Tchoupitoulas street, are both good houses; and the prices being less, they are sought after by those who wish to economise their expenses. There are several other respectable establishments, of which, like those last named, the limits of these pages will not permit a particular description.

THE GAS WORKS

Occupy a square fronting on St. Mary street four hundred and sixty-seven feet, with a depth of two hundred and thirty-five feet on Gravier and Perdido streets; which is enclosed by a substantial brick wall fourteen feet high. The site was selected by James H. Caldwell, Esq., to whom New Orleans is mainly indebted for this great undertaking, as well as for many others which stand as lasting eulogiums to his memory. In 1834, the original works were put in operation. Mr. Caldwell, at this time, had the exclusive privilege of lighting the city for thirty years. His were the fourth gas works in the Union, and the first west of the mountains. The first wrought-iron roof in this country, was erected over the retort house by Mr. C., and has served as a model for all since built. The largest cast iron tank ever constructed was also put up by him. It is fifty-one feet diameter and eighteen deep, and contains over two hundred thousand gallons of water. In 1835 Mr. Caldwell disposed of this property to the Gas Light and Banking Company; who, finding the buildings insufficient, constructed them anew. The present establishment was planned and erected under the superintendence of David John Rogers, in whose care it still continues to prosper. The works, finished in 1837, cost $150,000. The whole present value is $650,000.

These consist of a retort house on Gravier street, one hundred and seventeen by eighty feet, and parallel to which is the purifying house, one hundred and seventeen by fifty-two feet. On the rear is the chimney, constructed to resemble Trajan's pillar, one hundred and seven feet high; and presents a chaste specimen of classical architecture. There are three fifty feet gasometers, arranged along in the centre of the premises, capable of containing thirty thousand cubic feet each, built after the most approved workmanship, and considered to be superior to any others in this country. On Perdido street is a three story dwelling, thirty by seventy-five feet, for the workmen. The coal shed is one hundred and ninety by fifty-two feet. In addition to these are the blacksmith, carpenter, and other shops, necessary for advantageously conducting so extensive a business. The structures are all fire-proof, and every thing is kept in the neatest possible condition.

In addition to the works already described, and immediately in front of them, embracing nearly another square, two more gasometers, of equal

7

dimensions, together with the accompanying buildings, have been constructed during 1844—5.
These will enable the company to transmit the
gas through a distance of one hundred and fifty
miles of pipe, sufficient for the accommodation of
a half million of persons.

The gas is extracted from Pittsburgh coal—
after which the coke is sold for fuel, at about half
the price that is asked for the original coal.

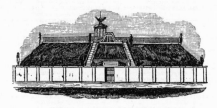

THE WATER WORKS.

In 1833, a company was incorporated under the
title of the "Commercial Bank of New Orleans,"
the principal object of which was to supply the
city with pure water from the Mississippi river.
To effect this object, an artificial mound was constructed on the square comprised within Richard,
Market, John the Baptist and Religious streets,
consisting of seventy thousand cubic yards of earth,
taken from the batture (deposit) of the river. The
work was completed during 1834—5. The
reservoir is constructed on the top of this mound.

It is two hundred and fifty feet square, built of brick, and divided into four compartments, measuring each one hundred and eighteen feet in the clear. The walls and bottoms forming the reservoir, are built with brick, and plastered with hydraulic cement. A pavilion of an octagonal form has been erected on the intersection of the partition walls, supported by eight pillars. It is about fifteen feet wide and ten high, and affords quite a commanding and pleasant prospect.

The reservoir is supplied with water from the Mississippi river, by plunge pumps, worked by a condensing engine, acting expansively on Bolton and Watt's plan. These pumps were adopted as the most efficacious, on account of the great quantity of matter held in suspension by the water. They are connected to a suction pipe sixteen inches in diameter, and about eight hundred feet long ; and to the main, descending into the reservoir, sixteen inches in diameter and six hundred feet long. The cylinder is twenty-five inches in diameter and six feet stroke, and is calculated to raise three millions gallons of water in twenty-four hours. The engine and pump houses are built of brick, and are situated on the lot forming the corner of Tchapitoulas and Richard streets.

The water is distributed through cast iron pipes, capable of sustaining a pressure of water of three hundred feet head. They vary from eighteen to six inches in diameter for the mains—but the greater part of them consist of the larger sizes, which have numerous ramifications of less dimensions. There are two mains from the reservoir; one of eighteen, the other of twelve inches bore, which are gradually reduced in size as the distance becomes greater from the source, or as circumstances may require. In 1836, water was first pumped into the reservoir. It can be delivered in the upper part of the city twenty-one feet, and in the lower sections, twenty-seven feet above the level of the soil.

The daily average consumption of water, during the year 1844, was one million gallons; and, from the comparative great capacity of the reservoir, sufficient time is allowed for the water to settle, in one of the four compartments, before it is drawn for the use of the city.

Much good might be achieved by a more enlarged operation of these works. The water is capable of being made fit for all domestic purposes, thus obviating the necessity for cisterns, the birthplace of millions of moschetoes, and, possibly the source of much sickness. For the purposes of bathing it is almost indispensable; and, for forming fountains, to cleanse the streets and to purify and cool the air, it may be rendered equally a convenience, a luxury, and an embellishment.

ARMORIES.

A room has been fitted up in Camp street, for which the substantial and well constructed walls of the old Camp street Theatre have been used— a building erected by James H. Caldwell, Esq., in 1822. This apartment, used as an armory for the Washington Battalion, is sixty by one hundred and twenty feet, and twenty-two feet high, and is decidedly one of the largest in New Orleans.

Another armory is located at the corner of Perdido and Baronne streets, in the upper part of the Carrolton Rail-Road depôt. Both of these armories are the depositories of arms, all kept in the best order, and disposed in various tasteful forms.

THE FIRE DEPARTMENT.

There are in New Orleans, fifteen engine, three hose, and one hook and ladder—in all nineteen companies. The city may justly boast of the energy and efficiency of this arm of safety. The members are exempt from military and jury duty ; and, after a certain term, are enrolled as honorary members, who are free from the performance of further service. The expenses of the department are defrayed by appropriations from the municipalities, and from fines imposed upon delinquent members.

The courage and bearing of these companies during a conflagration, are much to be admired. They proceed with that cool and determined spirit that shows a consciousness of their power in subduing the destructive element. An excellent and convenient supply of water, which is always at command, enables them promptly to extinguish the most dangerous fire.

———

MANUFACTURES

IN New Orleans, have, until recently been but little known. There are now however, several actively employed and well patronized branches of the manufacturing business; which, if not calculated to compete with those in other markets, answer a very good purpose for its own.

THE IRON FOUNDRY

Of Messrs. Leeds & Co. produces every variety of machinery, that steamboats and manufactories require for extensive operations. It has been established many years, at the corner of Foucher and Delord streets, occupies nearly a whole square, and is on as extensive a scale as any in the country. The business-like and prompt system practiced by the conductors, is known to all who require their aid upon the whole line of the Mississippi and its tributaries.

STEAM PLANING MILL,

Upon Carondelet Walk, has been in successful operation over four years. Lumber is landed from Carondelet Canal, which passes in front of the building.

STEAM SAW MILLS.

Of these there are two; one located in the third municipality, the other five miles below the city, and both upon the banks of the river. They can furnish lumber of almost any description in abundance.

ROPE WALKS.

There are several of these, in different parts of the city, where cordage may be manufactured, to any extent, demanded by the business of the place.

Besides these there are several Flour Mills, a Paper Mill, Sugar Refinery, Cotton Factories, &c., all in successful operation.

THE COTTON PRESSES.

THIS is the place of all others, for these extensive buildings, which, generally, occupy a square, and sometimes more. They are numerous and extensive establishments. A brief description of two of the most prominent, will serve for the whole, as they very much resemble each other in their construction.

THE LEVEE COTTON PRESS,

Erected by a company under that name, was completed in 1832, at a cost of $500,000. No architectural effect was aimed at in the façade, which is, however, neat and plain. This establishment can press about 200,000 bales per annum.

THE ORLEANS COTTON PRESS.

This vast establishment fronts on the Mississippi, running back on Roffignac and New Levee streets. The ground occupied is six hundred and thirty-two by three hundred and eight feet, and is nearly covered by the buildings. The whole was built according to designs made by Charles F. Zimpel, begun in 1833, and completed in 1835, at a cost, including the site, of $753,558. The front on the river, although having no pretensions to architectural effect, is still, from its location and extent, quite impressive. This press can store twenty-five thousand bales of cotton; and compresses, on an average, one hundred and fifty thousand bales per annum; but its capacity is much greater.

BANKS.

LOUISIANA STATE BANK.

This building was erected in 1822, at a cost, including the ground, of $55,000. The plan was from Latrobe, and Benjamin Fox the architect. It stands on the corner of Royal and Bienville streets, and presents rather a plain but neat external appearance. It is most substantially built; the lower story is heavily arched, and the banking apartments are completely fire-proof. Capital, $2,000,000.

THE MECHANICS' AND TRADERS' BANK,

Is situated on Canal street, occupying only an ordinary house, compared to some others, and requires no particular description. Capital $2,000,000.

7*

THE CITY BANK

Is a building of the Ionic order, situated in Camp, near Canal street, and designed by W. L. Atkinson, architect. Its construction was commenced in 1837, and finished in 1838, under the superintendence of J. Gallier, at a cost of about $50,000. The banking room is admired for its elegant simplicity. Capital $2,000,000.

THE GAS BANK.

This building, in St. Charles street, between Canal and Common streets, is so closely squeezed in among others, that it has little opportunity to show off the beauty it possesses. It was erected in 1839, under the superintendence of Sidel & Stewart, at an expense of about $25,000, ground $25,000, making $50,000, and is every way well calculated for a banking house. The original capital was $4,000,000, but it was reduced to $180,000, and by request of the stockholders, the banking privileges have been withdrawn by an act of the Legislature of 1845.

THE CANAL BANK

Has its entrance in the centre of the front on Magazine street, of a substantial granite building which stands on that and the corner of Gravier street. That portion of the edifice is very tastefully arranged after the designs of Dakin, the architect. It was erected in 1845. The residue of the structure is used for stores. Capital, $4,000,000.

THE BANK OF LOUISIANA.

Is a fine Ionic building at the south-west corner of Royal and Conti streets, surrounded by a handsome court. The whole edifice is well arranged, the banking room in particular, is admired for its good architectual effect, being 60 feet square, and of a proportionate height, with a fine gallery above. It was commenced by Bickle, Hamlet and Fox, builders, in 1826, and fin-

ished the following year, at a cost of $80,000
Capital $4,000,000.

BANKS' ARCADE

Occupies the front of a square on Magazine
street, between Gravier and Natchez streets, having a main entrance, from each of those last named,
to the Arcade, which divides the building through
the whole length—being three stories high, and
covered in with glass, to exclude rain and admit
the light. In the lower and second stories, are
offices of almost all descriptions—and the third is
appropriated mostly to sleeping rooms.

The bar-room, opening on Magazine street, is
100 by 60 feet, and 35 in height. It is hand-
somely embellished, has a gallery surrounding

the upper story, and is a popular place for public meetings. It will accomodate 5,000 people on such occasions. This building stands in the centre of business, and, consequently, is a place of great resort for merchants and others. Erected by Thomas Banks in 1833, Charles Zimple, architect.

CITY EXCHANGE.

This magnificent edifice, which is one of the greatest ornaments of the city, fronts on three streets—about 300 feet on St. Louis, and 120 each on Royal and Chartres street—the building being intended by the projectors to combine the convenience of a city exchange, hotel, bank, large ball rooms, and private stores.

The principal façade, on St. Louis street, may be generally described as being composed of the Tuscan and Doric orders. The main entrance is formed by six columns of the composite Doric

order.   Through this portico, access is had to the
vestibule of the Exchange, a handsome, though
simple hall, 127 by 40 feet.   This room is appropriated to general business, and constantly open
during waking hours.   You pass through this into
one of the most beautiful rotundas in America,
which is devoted exclusively to business, and is
open from noon to three o'clock P. M.   This fine
room is surrounded by arcades and galleries, always open to the public, (Sundays excepted,)and
its general appearance cannot fail to impress upon
the mind a most favourable idea of its grandeur
and beauty.   The dome is most tastefully laid off
in compartments, within which the magic pencils
of Canova and Pinoli have portrayed allegorical
scenes and the busts of eminent Americans, in
rich fresco—a style of painting comparatively
new in the United States.   The floors of the
gallery which engird the rotunda, and the winding
stairs leading to them, are of iron.

By a side entrance on St. Louis-street, access
is obtained to the second story ; the front of which,
on this street, is occupied by a suite of ball-rooms
and their dependencies.   The great ball room is
magnificent in its size and decorations.   The building also has a capacious entrance on Royal-
street, as a hotel that can accommodate 200
persons.   At the corner of Chartres street are the
public baths.   In the spring of 1840 this building

was nearly burnt down—but, in less than two years, it was completely restored to its original splendor.

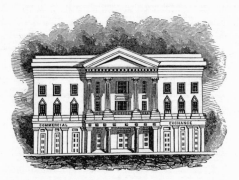

THE COMMERCIAL EXCHANGE.

This edifice is now being erected upon the south west corner of St. Charles and Perdido streets, fronting one hundred and three feet upon the former, and running one hundred upon the latter. The main part of the building is to be constructed of brick and stuccoed; the upper portion is purely Corinthian the lower entirely Tuscan. The principal entrance on St. Charles street, is by a portico supported by two Ionic pillars, and the same number of pilastres, composed of granite. The vestibule is eleven feet deep, which admits visitors by three separate doors into the exchange saloon, the most spacious apartment of the kind in the United States; it being seventy by one hundred feet, and twenty seven to the ceiling, which is supported by twelve well arranged and substantial pillars. At the rear of this public room are two others, intended for the accommodation of auctioneers, leaving only sufficient space on the left for the necessary offices and access to the second floor.

The structure shows three stories in front—on the second of which is the news room, expressly arranged for the occupation of the New Orleans Reading Room. This apartment is fifty-five by eighty-three feet, and thirty-seven to the ceiling; and is lighted by thirty-six windows. A portico, with a recess of eleven feet, occupies the immediate front, supporting the pediment by two Corinthian pillars, and an equal number of pilastres. Two rooms are set apart in connection with this establishment, one for the accommodation of captains of vessels, and one for that of sugar-brokers. On each side of the news-room are ranges of offices, to which admission is obtained by corridors on the inner side. Immediately over these, the third floor is arranged in the same manner. The intention of the company, under whose auspices this exchange is building, is, to furnish to the mercantile community a place solely for the transaction of business, similar to Lloyd's of London. There are to be no liquors sold on the premises. Mr.

Gallier is the architect, and builder, and the building and land cost $90,000.

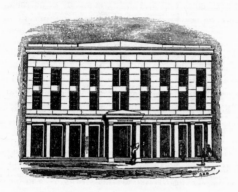

THE MERCHANTS' EXCHANGE,

Fronting on Royal street and Exchange Place, was erected by a joint stock company in 1835–6, from the designs and under the superintendence of Mr. Dakin, architect. Both fronts are of marble, in a plain and bold style. The cost of the erection was $100,000.

THE MERCHANTS' READING ROOM,

Entrance from Royal street and Exchange Place. This reading room occupied a spacious apartment in the second story of the Merchants' Exchange, and is under the patronage and control of the company interested in that building. It is generally supplied with most of the newspapers of the country, and has received a patronage quite equal to the extent of its accommodations.

THE NEW ORLEANS READING ROOMS

Occupy the second story of a spacious building on the corner of Common and St. Charles streets, opposite the Exchange and Verandah hotels. This is an enterprise started upon the plan of Galignani's, in Paris, and Lloyd's, in London—professing to supply the earliest commercial and general information. The fixtures are arranged with a degree of neatness and convenience that is extremely gratifying to the stranger, who has a spare hour to devote to reading. Here he can peruse the latest papers, not only from almost every section of the United States, but English, French, German, Mexican, Irish, Scotch, and Colonial, together with all the periodicals, to his heart's content. The merchant can see the prices current from nearly every part of the world; arrivals and departures of vessels and of travellers—sales of the great staples and merchandise and their prices, and many such matters of interest to the business man.

THE PUBLIC SCHOOLS,

IN each parish, have heretofore been placed under the management of a board of five administrators, who reported annually to the secretary of state the condition of those under their direction. This system has been adhered to, till very recently, in the first and third municipalities. In the second a change took place in 1841, which has proved to be so complete a revolution, is attended with such important results to this large portion of the city, and so extended its influence even to the neighboring parishes, that it is referred to with a degree of pleasure which can only be surpassed by our pride in its success.

In accordance with an act of the legislature, approved the 14th of February, 1841, authorizing the municipalities of New Orleans to establish public schools, the authorities of the second municipality set themselves at work with a will. They selected twelve of their fellow-citizens as a board of directors for public schools, together with a standing committee on public education, to whom were granted almost unlimited powers.

Zealous of acquitting themselves with honor, they at once looked to the fountain head, to New England, where the best schools in the country existed, and secured the aid of Mr. J. A. Shaw, who was perfectly conversant with all the improvements, and placed this efficient gentleman at the head of the department as superintendent. From a despairing beginning, in less than one year, the prospect seemed to be most cheering. Commencing with only thirteen children of each sex, it increased, in two years, to ten hundred and sixty-one in actual attendance—and nearly double that number enrolled.

Thus far these schools occupied rooms under the Methodist church in Poydras street, and a new building, called the Washington school, on Magazine, at the corner of Basin street; but since that, the undertaking has been continually extending, until it was found necessary to erect another structure, the Franklin school, on St. Charles street—all of which are now scarcely sufficient to answer the increasing demand for admission.

That, which at first was tested as an experiment, has proved to be a successful enterprise, producing an example which promises to have a beneficial influence over the southern method of education. It found strong opposition and prejudice to contend against, but these have subsided— and the children of the rich and the poor are seated side by side, sharing advantages and striving intellectually—the only distinction recognized among them—"teaching one, as well as informing the other, that adventitious wealth confers no superiority over the fortunate competitor, when engaged in a contest of the mind."

The third municipality school is under the charge of Mr. Geo. W. Harby. All the branches of a good education are taught here in the English, French and Spanish languages. Although this school is under excellent discipline, and has all the advantages of a classical and gentlemanly teacher, it still has labored under the old régime, and could have educated double the number that have attended it. That nothing stands still is as applicable to the intellectual as to the physical world. Already the spirit of improvement, that has done so much for the second municipality, is busy in the first and third—and though slowly, it is as sure, eventually, to push its way into them as water is to find its own level. Beside the public schools, there are many private seminaries of a high order, and conducted by teachers of ability, where the wealthy, who have objections to those above designated, may send their children for instruction.

The education of youth is of the utmost importance to a country—especially to one like this, that should be governed by the intelligence of its citizens. The portals to learning should be thrown wide open, equally to all—for upon knowledge is based the beautiful temple of liberty. Tear away this foundation and the fair edifice must fall. Cherish and support it, and freedom will become as permanent as our rocks, as ever-lasting as our hills.

PUBLIC SCHOOL LYCEUM AND SOCIETY LIBRARY.

The intention of this undertaking, is to establish a library for the benefit of the juvenile class of the second municipality, by the voluntary subscriptions and contributions of the scholars attached to the public schools, and by private donations. To advance this important object, the common council passed an ordinance organising the establishment, regulating and directing its proceedings, and tendering liberal advantages to encourage success in its operations. When $5000 are subscribed they are pledged to furnish rooms to accommodate the library—and, as soon as it amounts to $15,000, to purchase ground and erect suitable buildings. It also provides that, at a certain period, a chemical and philosophical apparatus shall be purchased, and lectures delivered once a week, during eight months of the year, by the most competent men in the country, on astronomy, geology, chemistry, natural and moral philosophy navigation, book-keeping, engineering, civil architecture and design, and such other useful branches as may be determined by the directors—who are the same as those of the public schools, with the mayor, recorder and aldermen as *ex-officio* members. The scholar paying twenty-

five cents a month, or three dollars a year, for
three years, is constituted a life member, and for
ever after may have access to this excellent institution. Such has been the success of this undertaking that a building will soon be provided, and
very little time will transpire before it will realize
all the advantages that its beginning promised. To
Samuel J. Peters, Esq., particularly, is this city
indebted for introducing and maturing this measure—and for generous presents, to many other
citizens and strangers, who have not permitted
their names to come before the world.

The growing popularity of the *"Peoples Lyceum,"* and of the *"Young Men's Literary Association,"* is noticed with no ordinary feelings of gra-
tification. These, commenced and continued by
the young, fostered and cherished by all—have
become a cheering sight to the eye of the christian, the patriot, and the philanthropist. Established upon judicious principles, tending to give a
wholesome direction and salutary stimulus to the
mind of their members, the moral influence may
be deemed of incalculable consequence to this
growing metropolis. History and science are the
leading objects of their inquiry, facilitated and
encouraged by the delivery of lectures, affording
not only instruction but recreation—creating a
taste for the rapid acquirement of knowledge—

giving a new impulse to the intellectual powers, and to the advancement of literature—all nobly contributing to the refinement and happiness of mankind. These, and others in the course of being established under the auspices of our most eloquent and learned literati, the city may class among the brightest of her jewels.

MEDICAL COLLEGE OF LOUISIANA.

This building is erected on a fine lot of ground, on the corner of Common and Philippa streets, granted to the college by a recent act of the legislature. It was designed by, and completed under the direction of Mr. Dakin, architect, whose reputation is a guaranty for its taste and elegance. The location is retired, and yet near all the public buildings and thoroughfares. The faculty of this institution are gentlemen of superior qualifications, enthusiastic in their zeal to give it the first place among the kindred establishments of the country. The advantages of New Orleans, for acquiring a practical knowledge of medicine and surgery, are superior to any city in the United States, especially for the study of all diseases peculiar to a southern climate. The facilities for prosecuting the study of anatomy and surgery are unrivalled. The school is well furnished with models, plates, casts, and every thing necessary for illustrations. The requisitions for graduation are those adopted by the best colleges. With these advantages presented to southern students, they will see the benefits resulting from an institution built up among them, conducted by gentlemen acquainted by experience with the wants of the country.

THE NATIONAL GALLERY OF PAINTINGS.

This establishment occupies rooms, expressly built for its accommodation, at 13 St. Charles street, and was opened in 1844, under the personal inspection of the proprietor, Mr G. Cooke, who is himself an artist of taste, and well known among the profession. The principal object was, to form a rallying point for the exhibition of the works of celebrated artists, both of foreign and American origin, and to dispose of such as might please the fancy of the public, at a certain fixed price. Here, visitors will have an opportunity of selecting copies and originals from a quarter that may be

8

relied upon, works both of the old masters, and of the best of the modern schools.

The proprietor is under obligations to a number of the gentlemen of this city, connoisseurs of painting, for the exhibition of some of the most prominent pieces. From R. D. Shepherd, Esq., he has a picture by Rothmel, representing De Soto discovering the Mississippi. If this artist should leave no other work, his reputation, as a genius of no ordinary ability, will remain as durable as the canvas on which he has pourtrayed the Spaniard and the "Father of Waters."

From James Robb, Esq., whose magnificent collection of modern paintings is better known in other cities than our own, the gallery has received its richest treasures, and most valuable contributions. The chef d'œuvre is from the pencil of a native artist now at Rome, Leutze; and illustrates this sentence in our Lord's prayer—"deliver us from evil." To speak of this gem in terms equal to its merits, would place it immeasurably above the estimation of the age in which we live. Aware that it may be considered presumption to compare living genius with the justly venerated names of the immortal dead, whose works, on account of their antiquity and intrinsic worth, are doubly valued—yet, at the risk of losing our little reputation in such matters, we venture the assertion that this picture of Leutze's will compare with the most beautiful of the Italian school, and is excelled by none in America, not excepting those of our lamented and talented Alston. This picture alone would make any gallery in Europe attractive, and the public are greatly indebted to Mr. Robb for the opportunity he has afforded them of seeing not only this, but many other brilliant productions.

Here, also, is a landscape of no ordinary excellence, by Boddington, an English artist, who has most successfully represented one of his native scenes, in a style of handling peculiarly true and free. Here may be seen four of Doughty's best landscapes, and several fine specimens from the pencils of Cole and Chapman. The portrait of Col. David Crocket, as large as life, in his forest costume, by Chapman, and two large altar pieces, copied from celebrated works in the Vatican —The Entombing of Christ, after Corregio—and The Crucifixion of St.Peter, after Guido—comprise a portion of the more recent additions to the gallery.

Among the most attractive performances, are The Wreck of the Medusa, The Roman Forum, and a Sketch of Rome—from the pencil of the proprietor. The first of these is very much admired— but, to the classical visitor, the last two are far more fascinating; calling up, as they do, with all their endearing associations, our happy school-day remembrances.

Much more might be said respecting this establishment, but the brevity of these pages will not
permit an indulgence of our wishes in a more
minute detail.

———

It is probably the general impression of strangers, suggested by the limited number and extent
of the public galleries of paintings in this city,
that there is, among us, an entire deficiency of a
proper taste for the fine arts. And we may, ourselves, inadvertantly have contributed to such an
impression, by representing our citizens as exclusively absorbed in commercial pursuits. It
must be received, however, with many abatements.
We have our artists, and not a few of them, who
are highly talented, and deservedly patronised.

There are choice collections of paintings in the
possession of several private gentlemen, other than
those already alluded to ; among which are many
valuable productions, not only of the modern but
ancient masters, purchased at enormous prices.

Among others, those owned by our highly esteemed fellow-citizens, Glendy Burke, H. R. W.
Hill, and Joseph M. Kennedy, Esqs., are well worth
a visit of the connoisseur and admirer of fine specimens of the arts, to which the known courtesy
of the proprietors will cheerfully afford ready
access. The only original painting of the famous

Wilkie in this country, is in the splendid collection of Mr. Burke.

Several fine specimens of original statues are in the possession of James Dick, and John Hagan, Esqs., which are not excelled by any collection in this country.

———

THE PRESS.

" What is it but a map of busy life,
Its fluctuations, and its vast concerns?"

THE diurnal press of this country, is not only a mighty political engine, but one of the utmost importance in a commercial and literary point of view. Its increase, within a few years past, like its extending liberty, is without a parallel, and almost beyond belief. Junius, in his peculiar manner, observes, that "they who conceive that our newspapers are no restraint upon bad men, or impediment to the execution of bad measures, know nothing of this country." The force of this remark applies nowhere better than to the Press of the United States.

Every enlightened American, who loves the constitution of his country, and correctly estimates its lofty principles, will lend his aid to preserve these invaluable privileges from the violation of power on the one hand, and the equally injurious outrages of popular licentiousness on the other.

The press of this city comes in for a portion of the credit that is attached to that of the country—more particularly for its elaborate commercial details and general literature. To embody the spirit of the age ; to relieve the grave by the gay ; and to embellish the useful by the amusing, is its daily task. The choicest of home and foreign literature is found in the leading issues from the New Orleans press. It is equally interesting to the merchant and the general reader ; and it preserves, above all its cotemporaries of other cities, a self-respect that does infinite credit to the gentlemen to whose hands the important trust is confided.

There are eight daily papers published in New Orleans—three of which may be rated as of the " mammoth" size ; the other five are smaller, but of sufficient dimensions to furnish the ordinary news of the day. They are as follows :

The Louisiana Courier is the only evening paper of the city, and is published in French and English. This is the pioneer, before referred to in this work, under the name of " La Moniteur." The Bee, also in French and English, and the Commercial Bulletin, in English, make up the three mammoth sheets. The Picayune, the Tropic, the Jeffersonian Republican, the Native American, and the New Orleans Times, are all in English. The New Orleans Price Current is a very useful publication, issued twice a week.

In addition to these, the Catholics and Protestants each have their weekly Journals, and the Medical faculty their bi-monthly Periodicals, edited by the most prominent members of the profession, and devoted to Medicine, and Collateral Sciences. They are intended to bring forth the industry and talents of the profession in the South, and to furnish the most recent information of its progress generally.

The subject of Organic Chemistry is that to which, at the present day, the eyes of all thinking members of the profession are directed, and upon which their hope of progress mainly depends,— the relations of chemical action to the functions of organized matter, the application of chemistry to physiology and pathology, are to be treated of as fully as present knowledge extends.

Such contributions to the noble science, in which these gentlemen have long been successful labourers, cannot fail to be properly estimated throughout the scientific world.

AMUSEMENTS.

At the commencement of the holydays, the city begins to put on a gay aspect. Visitors, from all parts of the habitable globe, have arrived, either on business or pleasure. A general round of balls, masquerades, soirées and parties begin, and are continued without intermission during the season. Theatres and operas, with their *stars* and *prima donnas,* circuses and menageries, bell-ringers and serenaders, are in full success—and New Orleans, filled with every description of amusement, from the top of the drama down to Judy and Punch. Strangers are surprised and delighted at the splendor that is carried out in these circles of pleasure. Our present object, however, is merely to describe the most conspicuous places of public resort.

ORLEANS THEATRE.

The site of this building was occupied by an edifice erected for dramatic performances in 1813, somewhat on the plan of the one now existing. This, which was built by a joint stock company, was burnt to the ground in 1816. Mr. John Davis afterwards became the sole proprietor, and began the erection of the present theatre.

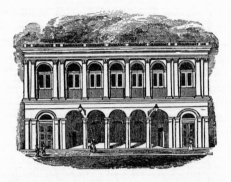

The building was opened by the first dramatic corps, ever in Louisiana directly from France, in November, 1819. The total cost of the edifice was about $180,000. The lower story is of the Roman Doric order, certainly not a pure specimen. The upper is what may be called the Corinthian composite. The interior and scenic arrangements of the house are excellent for seeing and hearing, having a pit, or parquette, quite elevated and commodious, with grated boxes at the side for persons in mourning; two tiers of boxes, and one of galleries above; the whole being of such a form as to afford the greatest accommodation to the spectators.

Nothing can exceed the decorum of the audience, except the brilliancy of the dress circle, which, on certain occasions, is completely filled

8*

with the beautiful ladies of our city, in full evening costume. The performances are in the French language, and the stock company always respectable. The orchestra is excellent. Melodramas and operas are perfectly got up at this house. The strict adherence to nature and history, in costume and manners, will never fail to please the man of taste who visits the Orleans theatre.

THE NEW ST. CHARLES THEATRE,

Like the phœnix, literally arose from the ashes of its predecessor. The first house was erected by the sole exertions of James H. Caldwell, Esq., in 1835, at the cost of $250,000, exclusive of the ground. It occupied one hundred and twenty-nine feet front by one hundred and eighty-six deep, and was seventy-six high. It held four thousand people, and was the fourth in size in the world— one at St. Petersburg, in Russia, another at Pescala, in Milan, and the third at San Carlos, in Naples, were those only which excelled it in size. It was destroyed by fire in 1842. That structure was styled "the Temple of the Drama," and the city had good reason to be proud of such an ornament.

The present building has a front of seventy-nine feet on St. Charles street, extends back one hundred and forty-nine, and is fifty-three high.

The main entrance and front wall are remains of the former establishment ; which, from the substantial workmanship, resisted the conflagration so effectually as to be made available the second time. Passing this memento, the spectator finds himself in the vestibule, thirty-four by twenty-three feet, from which a double flight of geometrically formed stairs ascend to the first tier. Here the pit is seen in a semi-circular shape. The centre box is but fifty-one feet from the foot lights, which brings the audience within a convenient distance of the stage. The depth of the front boxes to the rear is twenty-one feet. The proscenium presents an elevation of thirty-nine feet in the clear, by fifty in width. The upper circles of boxes possess the like advantage of the first, in respect to a distinct view of the performances.

The fronts of the boxes consist of an open balustrade, producing a novel, and agreeable effect. The dome is ornamented with sunken panels, suitably embellished with emblematic devices. A golden-fringed national drapery falls from the proscenium, displaying an ingeniously contrived allegory in the centre. Four columns sustain an ornamented entablature above, composed of a mixed style of architecture, and copied after those of the celebrated temple of Benares.

THE AMERICAN THEATRE,

Burnt on the 30th of July, 1842, was rebuilt and reopened on the 5th of December following, at a cost of $28,000. The building is ninety by one hundred and fifty feet, and sufficiently elevated for all the purposes of the drama, but irregular in its altitude. The depth of the stage is sixty feet, and the width of the proscenium thirty-eight. The house will accommodate over fifteen hundred persons. It stands near Lafayette square, on Poydras street; and, from its isolated position, presents quite an imposing appearance.

THE CIRCUS.

The company have fitted up the old depôt of the Carrolton rail-road, situated on the corner of Poydras and Baronne streets, as a place for exhibiting feats of horsemanship. As the buildings possess no especial interest beyond these performances, they require no particular description—but as this amusement has an attraction for almost every class of visitors, not to have referred to it might have been deemed an inexcusable oversight. There is a stage attached to this establishment; and farces and the ballet relieve the monotony of the sports of the ring.

THE PUBLIC SQUARES.

———

ALTHOUGH the public squares in New Orleans are neither numerous, nor upon a very extended scale, they are located with good taste, and are exceedingly convenient. The centres of Canal, Esplanade, Rampart and Basin streets have a very considerable space set apart for embellishments. Shrubbery, and other ornaments, are in progress, and they already begin to assume a beauty that does much credit to the city authorities. Nothing is more conducive to health than these pleasant resorts for wholesome exercise. Here the toil-worn citizen, the wearied scholar, and the confined artizan, may breathe the fresh air, enjoy a delightful morning or evening promenade, and catch an imaginary enjoyment, in miniature, of the blessed country.

WASHINGTON SQUARE is in the third municipality; is bounded by the Elysian Fields, Great-Men's, Casa Calvo and Frenchmen streets.—Though admirably situated, owing to the distance it stands from the denser portion of the city, it has not yet received those attentions which, at some future day, will render it a beautiful promenade.

PLACE D'ARMES, or *Parade Square*, is still more prominent, and is embellished with fine trees; but, as it is in the centre of the first municipality, with the public buildings on one front and the levee on the other, it is a matter of surprise that it has not been improved in a style worthy of the inhabitants; who, certainly are capable of appreciating the advantages of such delightful grounds.

CIRCUS PLACE is below Rampart street, with St. Claude on the rear, and St. Ann and St. Peter streets on its sides. This is the square once known as *Congo Park;* and is the place where the negroes, in olden times, were accustomed to meet to while away the cares of servitude. Many an old inhabitant can remember when he beheld these thoughtless beings dancing " Old Virginia never tire," or some other favorite air, with such a hearty gusto, upon the green sward, that the very ground trembled beneath their feet. Though the loud laugh, and the unsophisticated break-down, and double-shuffle of these primitive days have ceased, the spot yet remains, with all its reminiscences, as original as ever, with its capabilities of improvement still unimpaired.

LAFAYETTE SQUARE is decidedly the handsomest in the city. It is in the second municipality, and has St. Charles and Camp streets in front and rear, and several public buildings in its immediate neighborhood. It has a handsome and substantial iron railing around it, based upon well laid blocks of granite; is well laid off in regular walks, and is ornamented with beautiful and rare shrubbery, set out with geometrical accuracy on a raised surface, calculated to make it dry and pleasant.

ANNUNCIATION SQUARE, in the same municipality, is the largest, and, consequently, may some day become the most elegant in the city. Orange and Race streets are on its front and rear—and facing are some very tasteful private residences.

TIVOLI CIRCLE, as its name would imply, is a circular piece of land laid off as a public ground in Nyade, at the head of St. Charles street, and is intended to be ornamented.

THE OLDEN TIME.

Antiquity! the olden time! the hoary, venerable past! there is something sacred and soul subduing in the very sound of the words. Like the dying echo of the last tones of the departed, it is full of hallowed memories, and cherished associations, that haunt the inner chambers of the imagination, and linger with a mournful tenderness about the better feelings of the heart.

But what have *we* to do with Antiquity! They of the old World, who were grey with time and tottering with decay when, but yesterday, they saw us spring into being, laugh at our sometime boast of Antiquity; and well they may, for it is hardly as well substantiated as that of the simple boy who conceived himself the oldest person in the world, because he could not remember when he was born. Yet even we, in the New World, we, of its second or third generation, whose fathers were present at its birth and baptism, even *we* begin to talk gravely of the olden time, and to sigh and look sad over the melancholy grandeur of the past!

Well, be it so. In these stirring times, an age is shorter, and sooner achieved, than in those of "the

New Orleans in 1728.

MISSISSIPPI ou St LOUIS FLEUVE

QUAI

RUE DE BIENVILLE
RUE DE CONTI
RUE ST LOUIS
RUE DE TOULOUSE
RUE ST PIERRE
RUE D'ORLEANS
RUE ST ANNE
RUE DU MAINE
RUE ST PHILLIPPE
RUE DE L'ARSENAL

RUE CHARTRES
RUE ROYALE
RUE DE CONDE

PLACE ET ARMES

QUAI

CIMETIERE.

sluggish eld." Time is measured by events, and not by revolutions of the sun—by the progress of the mind, not by the slow sifting sands of the hour glass, and the amazing precocity of these latter days makes many ages out of a single century.

But what a vandal spirit is innovation! what a ruthless destroyer is this boasted modern improvement! It sweeps over the land with the energy of a new creation, demolishing and scattering whatever lies in its way, for the mere pleasure of reproducing it in a new and better form. It removes the ancient land marks, obliterates the last traces of ancient power and grandeur, levels mountains, fills up valleys, turns the courses of rivers, and makes all things bend to its iron will.

It works such rapid and magical changes in its headlong career, that few of us are able to point out what *has been*, or to predict with certainty what *will be* to morrow, Let us cherish then, with deeper veneration, the few relics that remain of the days of our fathers. Let us reverence Antiquity such as it is. Let the street commissioner, and the *improver* of old estates—

> Spare that ancient house,
> Touch not a single brick—

It is almost alone in its sombre dignity, in the midst of younger and gayer edifices, that have swept New Orleans *as it was*, into the shade of oblivion. Antiquity—I mean, if I may be allowed the

Irish figure of speech—modern Antiquity, her countenance grave with sorrow, with here and there a furrow upon her yet ample brow, protests against the desecration of all that *was* dear and sacred. Standing on the verge of annihilation, with "one foot in the grave," and conscious that her days are numbered, her dissolution nigh at hand, she commands, she implores us to save one memento of the past, one legible souvenir of "the days of auld lang syne" And here it is.

THE OLD SPANISH BUILDING

At the corner of Royal and St. Anne streets, is delineated in the above engraving as it now stands —and long may it remain as a memorial of other times.

Thirty years ago—which, comparatively would take us back three centuries in any European city—thirty years ago, one might have seen from that spot, then the centre of the city, long perspective street-scenes of a similar character. INNOVATION has now done her work—has absolutely trodden the city of the last century under her feet.

The Casa Blanca, at the corner of Bienville and Old Levee Streets, has also escaped the general demolition. It was once the courtly residence of Bienville, the first governor of Louisiana—the seat of power, and the centre of wealth, beauty and fashion in the province. It is still on its old foundation, standing "alone in its glory," and the spirit of innovation has so far respected its ancient uses, that it is still a treasury of wealth, and a conservatory of the *sweetness* of our favored clime—a store house of sugar and molasses!

Environs of New Orleans.

EXCURSIONS.

In consequence of the level surface of the country in the environs of New Orleans, a great variety of scenery cannot be expected—yet, on the northern shore of lake Pontchartrain, the ground is somewhat higher and rolling, and affords very pleasant positions. Although not formed like the prolific north and west, in hill and dale, cliffs and cascades, alternately varying and beautifying the landscape, yet there are charming rides and rambles in the neighorhood of this city, of which a more minute account will be given under their respective heads, which follow.

Carrolton, a distance of six miles by the rail-road, is an exceedingly pleasant resort. The line, for nearly a third of the way, passes through the suburbs of the city, and is dotted on either side with beautiful residences—the remainder passes through cultivated fields, pleasant pastures, and delightful wood-lands. The road, like the country, is perfectly level, and kept in the finest condition. At the end of the route is situated the village; which is principally composed of tastfully built cottages, constructed in every variety of architecture that suited the individual fancy of the owner. Opposite the rail-road depôt, is one of the handsomest and most extensive public gardens, that is to be found in the vicinity of New Orleans. A race course is near by ; and the strolls around are quit cheering to those who fly from the turmoil and dust of the metropolis.

THE SHELL ROAD of the Canal and Banking Company, affords an agreeable ride to lake Pontchartrain, also a distance of six miles. The highway runs on the margin of the canal, and is not excelled by any road in the United States. It is the great resort for every species of pleasure vehicle that the city furnishes ; and here may be seen, on an afternoon, all grades of society, from the gay sportsman, mounted on his fast trotter, to the sober citizen, who sallies forth on his ambling poney, all of whom appear to realize an equal share of enjoyment. A line of comfortably arranged barges also ply on the canal from the lake, at which place a convenient hotel is established. Half way on this road, between the city and the lake, is the highly celebrated Metarie race track.

THE PONTCHARTRAIN RAIL-ROAD, runs to the lake from which it derives its name, from the head of Elysian Fields street, a distance of five miles. It is a very pretty ride. This route communicates with the great nothern mail line, which goes by the way of Mobile—and all the steamboats,

that traverse the lakes to the various villages and
landings that surround it, make this their general
starting point. From here, a passage is obtained
to Biloxi, which, the reader will recollect, was the
first spot settled by the French in this portion of
the world; and, from that circumstance, will natu-
rally excite the curiosity of the intelligent way-
farer. At the termination of this rail-road is a
first-rate hotel for the accommodation of visitors.
Here is good bathing, fishing and shooting; and,
beneath the shade of the trees, the breeze from
the water is delightfully refreshing.

THE MEXICAN GULF RAIL-ROAD, runs from Elysi-
an-Fields street, on Good Children street, towards
Lake Borgne. There are twenty eight miles of
this road now in operation. When finished, it
will afford considerable facilities to commerce, besides great benefit to the citizens, conveying them,
in about one and a half hours, to the refreshing
breeze of the ocean—where fish, oysters and
game may be found in abundance. No doubt it
will compete with the most favored watering
places of Bay St. Louis, Pass Christian, Boloxi,
&c. It will also be a great accommodation to the
planters in the neighbourhood—who already, so far
as it goes, have given it good encouragement.
This road has recently been purchased of the
State, by A. Gordon and Co., who, availing themselves of about 22 miles of the Nashville rail-

9

road iron, are bringing this work to a rapid completion.

THE ROAD OF BAYOU ST. JOHN, which follows the sinuosities of that stream, and reaches lake Pontchartrain at the site of the old fort St. John, after travelling the distance of about six miles, presents a very pleasant drive. Returning by the new Shell road before mentioned, it varies the route without adding much to the distance.

MACDONOUGH stands on the banks of the river opposite to New Orleans; and the crossing, in the hottest weather, is generally accompanied by a slight breeze, rendered cool and pleasant by the mighty current of the river, which comes from the icy springs of the Alleghanies and the Rocky mountains. The village, of itself, possesses no great beauty—but the country, the beautiful country is all around—and the noise and confusion of the city no longer annoy you. The great attraction at this spot is in visiting the United States marine hospital, one of the handsomest structures in Louisiana, which stands a little above.

ALGIERS adjoins, and seems a part of Macdonough. This is the great work-shop of New Orleans, for the building and repairing of vessels. It has its dry docks, and other facilities for the most extensive operations. In business times, it presents a scene of activity that is seldom observed in any other part of these regions, and reminds one of the bustling and enterprise of the North. The period has been when Algiers prescribed the law, *vi et armis*, to the city itself—but the day and the disposition, have happily long since passed away.

GRETNA, on the same shore, is nearly two miles further up the river, and stands opposite Lafayette. The whole distance is spotted with comfortable residences, principally inhabited by the owners of the adjoining grounds, and the walk from Algiers to this village is very gratifying to one partial to such exercise. There is a steamboat constantly plying from here to the city, which affords a desirable excursion of nearly three miles, touching at Lafayette in its passage each way. The village has a rural appearance, is regularly laid out, and exhibits some neat tenements. The forest approaches quite near ; and, the idea that one may so easily lose himself in the neighbouring woods, gives to the place a touch of romance which only the denizens of a crowded city know how to appreciate. From the great number of cattle observed along the shore, it would seem as if there was no necessity of diluting the milk for the New Orleans market, unless the milkmen be tea-total temperance men, and take this method to introduce the inhabitants gradually to a taste for water.

THE RACE COURSES. There are three of these

in the vicinity of this city. The *Louisiana,* near lake Pontchartrain; the *Metairie,* near the Shell road; and the one at Carrolton. These are as well patronised as any in the country, and, in the racing season, the inhabitants of the neighbouring states, from a great distance, flock hither to participate in the sports of the turf. Much praise has been bestowed upon the arrangements on these occasions. Even here, as in many other countries, the ladies, by their presence, have given them countenance and encouragement—and the course usually is "gemmed by the rich beauty of the sunny south."

THE BATTLE GROUND, (formerly known as "the Plains of Chalmette,") the very naming of which causes the bosom of an American to swell with patriotic pride, lies five miles below the city. It may be approached either by the Grand Gulf railroad, or by a good highway along the levee, the new Convent and United States barracks being within full view. But first it may be necessary to look briefly at the historical facts which give celebrity to the spot.

Early in December, 1814, the British approached New Orleans, about 8000 strong, by the way of the lakes Borgne and Pontchartrain. Their passage into the lake was opposed by a squadron of gun-boats under Lieut. Jones. After a spirited conflict, in which the killed (500) and the wounded of the enemy exceeded the whole American force, he was compelled to surrender to superior numbers.

On the 21st of Dec. four thousand militia arrived from Kentucky and Tennessee, under General Jackson. On the 22nd, the enemy having previously landed, took a position near the Mississippi, eight miles below the city. On the evening of the 23d, the Americans made a furious attack upon their camp, and threw them into disorder, with five hundred of their men killed. The enemy rallied ; and Gen. Jackson withdrew his troops, and fortified a strong position six miles below the city, supported by batteries on the west side of the river. Here he was unsuccessfully assailed on the 28th of Dec. and 1st of Jan., the enemy losing two hundred to three hundred men. In the mean time both armies received reinforcements.

The decisive battle was fought on the 8th day of Jan. 1815. The American right was on the river, running in a right angle to the wood. A redoubt was raised (which is still visible) strengthened by bales of cotton along the whole line. The enemy were about a half mile lower down, on a parallel line, their head quarters resting on the river, near three large oaks which still mark the spot. The scene is distinct, and this is *the battle ground*.

The British commenced the assault at day light.

As they approached the works, sixty deep, many were killed by grape shot; but, when they came within musket range, a destructive stream of fire burst forth from the American lines. Our troops were placed in two ranks, the rear loading while the front fired, thus pouring an incessant peal— which, from Kentucky and Tennessee riflemen, was most deadly. While leading on the troops of the enemy, Gen. Pakenham, the chief in command, was killed; Gen. Gibbs, the second in command, was wounded mortally; and Gen. Keene severely. Without officers to direct them, the troops halted, fell back, and soon fled in confusion to their camp. In a little over an hour, two thousand out of eight thousand veterans lay dead upon the field, while the Americans had but seven killed and six wounded—a disproportion unparalled in the history of warfare. Gen. Lambert, upon whom the command then devolved, after one more unsuccessful attempt to assault, availed himself of a truce of twenty-four hours to bury the dead, made good his retreat—which Gen. Jackson felt no disposition to molest, as he was resolved to hazard none of his advantages. Thus was New Orleans saved from the hands of an invading enemy whose War cry was—"Beauty and Booty."

The British lost during the month they were in Louisiana, more than three thousand three hundred and fifty in killed, while the loss of the

Americans was not two hundred. The wounded of the enemy must have been much less, on account of the sure aim of the backwoodsmen· The greater portion of our army were plain honest farmers—who knew nothing of battle—they heard that their country was in danger—the country which gave a home to them, and their children, and they flew to its defence,—drove the invaders from their shores, and then returned to their homes to till the ground.

It is not a matter of surprise—though the battle is without a parallel in the history of the world— that even "invincibles," were so dreadfully routed by undisciplined backwoodsmen defending their native soil, with their wives and children behind them.

A jaunt to these grounds is a sort of pilgrimage, that no stranger will, that no citizen can neglect. Not to have seen the field of this great victory, would be a reflection upon the taste, not to say the patriotism of any who should visit our city. The ground it is true, presents few memorials to remind the patriotic visitor of the deadly strife. There is no proud monument, towering to the sky, to mark the place where the great victory was won. But he beholds the consequences wherever he turns his eye, and he feels them—deeply feels them in every throb of his heart. Those born upon the soil, and those who participated in the struggle, have reason to be proud of the spot, and to cherish the memory of that eventful day. If there is no lofty structure of granite or marble, to perpetuate the glorious achievement, it has a holier, a more enduring memorial in the heart of every true American, which thrills with lofty pride at every allusion to it, as did the ancient Greek at the name of Marathon, or the Spartan at that of Thermopylæ.

TRAVELLING ROUTES.

———

THE facilities which this metropolis affords for reaching any accessible portion of the world, particularly all sections of the union, are not excelled. Steam and sailing ships of the first class, hold commercial intercourse with almost every nation. Steam-boats, with accommodations equal to the best regulated hotels, are plying through every river and bayou. Four to five thousand miles can be achieved, in those floating palaces, with perfect ease, and comparative safety.

The principal routes between the north and the south are here given, as also the intermediate places, together with those inland most frequented by the traveller and the man of business, and the distances carefully noted as they diverge, in their various directions. Beside the four annexed routes to New York, there are several that lead to favorite watering places, and other points attractive to travellers of leisure, which it would be quite impracticable to lay down in a work of this kind.

9*

They can always obtain information of these resorts, from intelligent companions on the road, that will prevent their deviating much from the point they wish to attain. The distances on the river have been corrected agreeably to the latest survey. The other routes conform to the most approved authorities ; and, frequently, have been corrected by personal observation, with the utmost care and attention.

ROUTE 1.—*From New Orleans to New York, via Pittsburg, Pa., by Steamboat.*				Miles.
		Miles	Princeton, Miss.,	10	510
			Columbia, Ark.,	45	555
			Bolivar, Miss.,	53	608
New Orleans to Carrolton,	6		Napoleon, (Arkansas,)	12	620
Red Church,	20	26	Victoria,	20	640
Bonne Carre Church,	16	42	Delta,	66	706
Jefferson College,	22	64	Helena,	10	716
Donaldsonville,	19	83	Sterling,	10	726
Louisiana Institute,	12	95	Peyton, Miss.,	12	738
St. Gabriel Church,	12	107	Commerce,	33	771
Plaquemine,	10	117	Buck Island,	6	777
Baton Rouge,	23	140	Memphis, Tenn.,	21	798
Port Hudson,	25	165	Devil's Race Ground,	34	832
Bayou Sara,	11	176	Randolph, Tenn.,	33	865
Tunica Bend,	27	203	Fulton, Tenn.,	11	876
Red River, cut off,	33	236	Plumb Point,	10	886
Fort Adams, Miss.,	11	247	Ashport,	12	898
Homo Chitta River, Miss.,	10	257	Needham's Cut-off,	8	906
Ellise Cliffs, Miss.,	26	283	Walker's Bend,	31	937
Natchez, Miss.,	18	301	Riddel's Point,	18	955
Rodney, Miss.,	31	332	New Madrid, Mo.,	10	965
Bruinsburg, Miss.,	12	344	Mills' Point,	42	1007
GrandGulf, (big black) Miss	10	354	Columbus, K.,	15	1022
Carthage, Miss.,	25	379	Cairo, (Mo'th Ohio R'r.) Il,	18	1040
Warrenton, Miss.,	19	398	Trinity,	6	1046
Vicksburg, Miss.,	10	408	America, Il.,	5	1051
Old River, (Yazoo), Miss.,	12	420	Caledonia, Il.,	3	1054
Tompkins' Bend,	46	466	Fort Massac, Il.,	23	1077
Providence, La.,	15	481	Paducah, (M. Tenn R'r) K.	8	1085
Bunch Bend,	19	500	Smithfield, (M. Cum'd) K.	1	1097

	Miles.			Miles.
Galconda, Il.,	18	1115	Levana, O., and Dover, K., 2	1592
Tower Rock,	15	1130	Ripley, O., 3	1595
Cave in the Rock,	5	1135	Charleston, K., 5	1600
Battery Rock,	9	1144	Maysville, K., and Aber-	
Shawneetown, Il.,	12	1156	deen, O., 7	1607
Raleigh, K.,	6	1162	Manchester, O., 11	1618
Wabash River,	6	1168	Vanceburg, K., 16	1634
Carthage, K.,	7	1175	Alexandria, 18	1652
Mount Vernon, Ia.,	13	1188	Portsmouth, O., 2	1654
Henderson, K.,	28	1216	Concord, O., 8	1662
Evanville, Ia.,	12	1228	Greenupsburg, K., 13	1674
Owensboro, K.,	36	1264	Burlington, O., 23	1697
Rockport,	12	1276	Guyandot, Va., 7	1704
Troy, Ia.,	16	1292	Galliopolis, O., 35	1739
Cloverport,	21	1313	Point Pleasant, 3	1742
Stephensport, K., and			Letart's Rapids, 30	1772
Rome, Ia.,	10	1323	Belleville, Va., 28	1800
Fredonia,	34	1357	Troy, O., 5	1805
Leavenworth,	2	1359	Belpie and Blennerhas-	
Mauckport, Ia.,	14	1373	sett's Island, 12	1817
Brandenburg,	3	1376	Parkersburg, Va., 2	1819
West Point, K.,	18	1394	Vienna, Va., 5	1824
Portland, K., and New			Marietta, O., 6	1830
Albany, Ia.,	20	1414	Newport, O., 15	1845
Shippingport,	1	1415	Sistersville, 27	1872
Louisville, K.,	3	1418	Wheeling, Va., 40	1912
Jeffersonville, Ia.,	1	1419	Warren, 9	1921
Westport, K.,	19	1438	Wellsburg, Va., 6	1927
Bethlehem,	6	1444	Steubenville, 7	1934
New London.	6	1450	Welleville, O., 20	1954
Madison, Ia.,	7	1457	Georgetown, 7	1962
Port William, K.,	14	1471	Beaver, 13	1974
Vevay, Ia., and Ghent K.,	8	1479	Economy, 12	1986
Warsaw, K.,	11	1490	Middletown, Pa., 8	1994
Rising Sun, Ia.,	20	1510	Pittsburg, Pa., 10	2004
Bellevue,	2	1512	Warrenton, by Canal 47	2051
Petersburg,	7	1519	Blairsville, do 28	2079
Aurora,	2	1521	Johnstown, do 29	2108
Lawrenceburg,	3	1524	Hollidaysburg, by rail road, 37	2145
North Bend,	7	1531	Alexandria, by Canal, 26	2171
Cincinnatti, O., and Cov-			Lewiston, do 57	2228
ington and Newport, K.,	17	1548	Newport, do 36	2264
Columbia,	8	1556	Harrisburg, do 26	2290
Richmond,	13	1569	Philadelphia, by rail road 101	2391
Point Pleasant,	4	1573	Trenton, do 28	2419
Macon,	4	1577	Brunswick, do 27	2446
Neville,	3	1580	Jersey City, do 31	2477
Mechanicsburg, O.,	3	1583	New York, by steamboat, 1	2478
Augusta,	7	1590		

ROUTE 2.—*New Orleans to New York, via St. Louis, Chicago and Buffalo, [see route 1,] to Mouth of the Ohio, Steamboat to St. Joseph.*

	Miles.			Mies.
Mouth of Ohio,	1040	Middle Sister Island, do	20	1900
Elk Island,	8 1048	North Bass Island. do	10	1910
Dogtooth Island,	8 1056	Cunningham's Island, do	10	1920
English Island,	15 1071	Sandusky, O., do	12	1932
Cape Giradeau, Mo.,	12 1083	Cleaveland, O. do	54	1986
Bainbridge, Mo,, and		Fairport, O., do	30	2016
Hamburg, Il.,	10 1093	Ashtabula, O., do	32	2048
Lacouse's Island,	31 1124	Fairview, Pa., do	28	2076
Kaskaskia River,	15 1139	Erie, Pa., do	11	2087
River au Vases,	10 1149	Bugett's Town, Pa., do	17	2104
St. Genevieve, Mo.,	9 1158	Portland, N. Y., do	18	2122
Fort Chartres Island,	10 1168	Dunkirk, N. Y., do	18	2140
Rush Island,	10 1178	Cattaraugus, N. Y., do	13	2153
Herculaneum, Mo.,	10 1188	Sturgeon Point, N. Y., do	10	2163
Harrison, Il.,	1 1189	Buffalo, N. Y., do	16	2179
Merrimack River	11 1200	Williamsville, by rail road,	10	2189
Carondelet, Mo.,	13 1213	Pembroke, do	16	2205
St. Louis, Mo.,	7 1220	Batavia, do	14	2219
Alton, Il.,	22 1242	Rochester, do	25	2244
Illinois River,	15 1257	Canandagua, do	25	2269
Monroe,	5 1262	Geneva, do	16	2285
Guilford,	10 1272	Waterloo, do	7	2292
Montezuma,	20 1292	Seneca Falls, do	4	2296
Augusta,	15 1307	Cayuga, do	3	2299
Meridosia,	23 1330	Auburn, do	9	2308
Beardstown,	16 1346	Skaneatelas do	7	2315
Havana,	27 1373	Marcellus, do	6	2321
Pekin,	34 1407	Onondaga, do	8	2329
Peoria,	7 1414	Manlius, do	12	2341
Henry,	10 1424	Oneida, do	18	2359
Columbia,	10 1434	Utica, do	22	2381
Lacon,	4 1438	Herkimer, do	16	2397
Hennepin,	18 1456	Little Falls, do	7	2404
Chippeway,	16 1472	Caughnawaga, do	33	2437
Shippingport,	2 1474	Amsterdam, do	10	2447
Dresden,	46 1520	Schenectady, do	15	2462
Mount Joliet,	15 1535	Albany, do	15	2477
Lockport,	6 1541	New Baltimore, steamboat.	15	2492
Chicago, Il.,	29 1570	Kinderhook landing, do	4	2496
Michigan City, Ind.,	52 1622	Hudson, do	9	2505
New Buffalo, M.,	12 1634	Catskill, do	5	2510
St. Joseph, M.,	28 1662	Clermont, do	9	2519
Detroit, by rail road,	200 1862	Redhook, upper landing,	2	2521
Fighting Island, by steam-		Redhook, lower do	3	2524
boat	12 1874	Rhinebeck, do	7	2531
Amhurstsburg, U. C., do	6 1880	Esopus, do	1	2532
		Hyde Park, do	9	2541
		Poughkeepsie, do	5	2546
		New Hamburg, do	8	2554
		Newburg, do	7	2561
		Fishkill, do	1	2562
		New Windsor, do	1	2563

by steam boat

	Miles.	
Cold Sping, by steam boat,	3	2566
West Point, do	3	2569
St. Anthony's Nose, do	7	2576
Fort Fayette, do	5	2581
Stony Point, do	1	2582
Haverstraw, do	4	2586
Sing Sing, do	3	2589
Tarrytown, do	6	2595
Phillipstown, do	10	2605
Fort Independence, do	4	2609
Fort Washington, do	2	2611
Fort Lee, do	1	2612
Manhattanville, do	2	2614
New York, do	8	2622

ROUTE 3.—*New Orleans to New York, via Wheeling and Baltimore.*

To Wheeling, by steam boat, [see route 1.]		1912
Cumberland, by stage,	131	2043
Hancocktown Md, railroad	39	2082
Williamsport, Md., do	27	2109
Frederickstown, Md., do	27	2136
Poplar, Md., do	20	2156
Ellicott's, Md., do	17	2173
Baltimore, Md,, do	10	2183
Havre de Grace. Del., do	31	2214
Wilmington, Del., do	36	2250
Philadelphia, Pa., do	26	2276
New York, (see route 2,)	88	2364

ROUTE 4.—*New Orleans to New York, Mail line.*

	Miles.	
Point Pontchartrain, by rail road,	5	
Fort Pike, by steamboat	21	26
Bay St. Louis, do	33	59
Biloxi, do	31	90
Pascagoula, Miss., do	20	110
Cedar Point, Al., do	26	136
Mobile, Al., do	28	164
Junction of Alabama and Tombigkbe river do	65	229
Claiborne, do	72	301
Black Bluff, do	46	347
Dale Town, do	35	382
Canton, by steam boat.	14	396
Portland, do	29	425
Cahaba, do	21	446
Selma, do	18	464
Benton, do	35	499
Vernon, do	39	538
Loch Ranza do	6	544
Washington, do	16	560
Montgomery do	12	572
Chehaw, Al., by railroad,	40	612
Covington, Ga., by stage,	155	767
Augusta. Ga., by railroad,	121	888
Charleston, S. C., do	136	1024
Wilmington, N. C. by steamboat,	220	1244
Weldon, N. C., railroad,	170	1414
Richmond, Va., do	124	1538
Washington City, do	122	1660
Baltimore, Md., do	40	1700
New York, (see route 3.)	181	1881

ROUTE 5.—*New Orleans to Fort Gibson by steam boat.*

Arkansas river, (see route 1)	620	
Arkansas,	62	682
New Gascony,	71	753
Pine Bluffs,	25	778
Little Rock,	150	928
Lewisburg,	66	994
Scotia,	50	1044
Morrison's Bluff,	33	1077
Van Beuren,	72	1149
Fort Smith,	8	1157
Fort Coffee, Mo.,	10	1167
Fort Gibson,	84	1251

ROUTE 6.—*New Orleans to Balize, and Gulf of Mexico, by Steam boat.*

Battle Ground,	5	
English Turn,	6	11
Fort St. Leon,	5	16
Poverty Point,	18	34
Grand Prairie,	27	61
Fort St. Philip,	9	70
South West Pass,	9	79
South Pass,	2	81
Pass a' l'Outre,	2	83
Balize,	4	87
Gulf,	5	92

Miles.   Miles

ROUTE 7.—*New Orleans to the Raft on Red River, by Steamboat*

Mouth of Red River,	236	
Black River,	28	264
Bayou Saline,	20	284
Alexandria,	56	340
Regolet de Bondieu,	18	358
Bayou Cane,	36	394
Natchitoches,	24	418
Bastian's Landing,	40	458
The Raft,	40	498

ROUTE 8.—*New Orleans to Pittsburg, Miss., by Steamboat.*

Mouth of Yazoo River, Miss.,	420	
Satartia,	66	486
Liverpool,	5	491
Manchester,	25	516
Tchula,	88	604
Marion,	37	641
Mouth of Yalo Busha river,	33	674
Cochuma,	38	712
Pittsburg,	27	739

ROUTE 9.—*New Orleans to Nashville, Tenn., by Steamboat.*

Cumberland river,	1097	
Eddyville, K.,	56	1153
Canton,	20	1173
Dover, Tenn.,	30	1203
Palmyra,	31	1234
Red River,	6	1240
Harpeth River,	20	1260
Nashville,	40	1300

ROUTE 10—*New Orleans to Florence, Ala., by Steamboat.*

Tennessee River,	1085	
Petersville, Tenn.,	71	1156
Reynoldsburg,	36	1192
Perryville,	42	1234
Carrollville,	27	1261
Coffee,	26	1287
Savannah,	9	2196
Waterloo,	25	1321
Bear Creek,	12	1333
Colbert's Ferry, Tenn.,	14	1347
Florence, Al.,	24	1371

GENERAL INDEX.

DATE DUE